Living
the Advent-Christmas
Seasons

Compiled and edited by Edie Staf

Celebrating
the Advent-Christmas
Seasons

by Mary Lewis

Revised and Enlarged

BOOKS & MEDIA

Boston

Library of Congress Cataloging-in-Publication Data

Living and celebrating the Advent-Christmas seasons. — Rev. and enl. 1988
    p. cm.
    Contents: Living the Advent-Christmas seasons / compiled and edited by Edie Staf — Celebrating the Advent-Christmas seasons / by Mary Lewis.
    ISBN 0-8198-4419-5 (pbk.)
    1. Advent—Prayer-books and devotions—English.   2. Christmas—Prayer-books and devotions—English.   3. Devotional calendars—Catholic Church.   4. Catholic Church—Prayer-books and devotions—English.   I. Living the Advent-Christmas seasons. 1988.
II. Lewis, Mary, 1926-   Celebrating the Advent-Christmas seasons. 1988.
BX2170.A4L58   1988
263'.91—dc19

                                                    87-32905
                                                    CIP

Printed and published in the U.S.A. by Pauline Books & Media, 50 St. Paul's Avenue, Boston, MA 02130.

http://www.pauline.org   E-mail: PBM_EDIT@INTERRAMP.COM

Pauline Books & Media is the publishing house of the Daughters of St. Paul, an international congregation of women religious serving the Church with the communications media.

5 6 7 8 9 10   02 01 00 99 98 97

Contents

Living the Advent Season

First Week of Advent

Second Week of Advent

Third Week of Advent

December 17 to December 24

Living the Christmas Season

Christmas Novena: December 16 – 24

Celebrating the Advent-Christmas Seasons

Introduction

The mystery and the wonder of Christmas are an annual reminder of the awesome and unselfish love that God has shown his people. As we pause and ponder the marvelous reality of the coming of God's own Son amid the stark poverty of Bethlehem, we are lifted outside of ourselves and our own concerns. We are elevated to a new appreciation of and gratitude for the saving love and Providence of our Lord and God.

Despite the shopping-day countdown and the other mundane implications which our modern culture has attached to the season, Christmas is intended to be savored as a taste of the eternal. Preceded by the peaceful and meaningful Advent season, Christmas is meant by God to be a deeply spiritual and salvific moment.

Advent is a time of renewal, conversion, change. It is a time to turn away and break off from the many obstacles to spiritual growth. It is a time to strengthen our bonds with God and with those whom his Providence has placed in our lives. One means to use is the sacrament of Reconciliation, which God has given us to arrive at forgiveness of sin and to acquire the grace to achieve true interior conversion.

Although most will readily recall that Christmas is a "family time," perhaps not so many are aware that Advent is, too. Included in this book are a number of suggested customs and projects intended to spark family sharing in the genuine spirit of hope and expectation, love and joy, which are characteristic of Advent.

While Christmas parties and similar holiday festivities are not totally contrary to the spirit of Advent, it is far more appropriate to give priority to practices which emphasize the spiritual meaning. A day dedicated to prayer, charitable activities aimed at reaching out to others, family projects that cultivate greater unity and love—these are ways to sanctify and make the most out of Advent.

If Advent is spent in a genuinely Christian manner, Christmas will be that much more beautiful. Although no parent can ignore the pleadings and wistful desires of little people "making a list and checking it twice," neither can the dedicated and wise parent overlook the fact that the material dimension must be offset by the spiritual. Never before has there been more need of emphasizing the genuine meaning and message of Christmas. How beautiful it is to hear parents standing with their children before the manger scene recounting the events of long ago which are so pertinent to our present era. The wonder on the children's faces, the spontaneous desire to welcome Jesus and to converse with him and Mary and Joseph, are among the first expressions of youthful faith.

Perhaps more than any other time of the year, the Advent-Christmas seasons remind us that our faith in God, our hope in his promises and our love for him and each other, are the greatest wealth we possess. Many still "walk in darkness," because they know little or nothing about Jesus Christ and his redeeming love for us. Perhaps we will be moved to share more readily and more widely the gifts God has blessed us with. In this way, we best repay him who has made Christmas what it is—a celebration of life and of love.

*Living
the
Advent Season*

Advent

Advent—
 a time of waiting
   of expectancy
   of eager longing
     for Messiah
     for One who can
       heal us
       save us
       make us whole.

The secret—
     in awaiting
     the Advent of God
     is poverty of spirit—
       recognition of our nothingness
         helplessness
         hopelessness
           to save ourselves.

We—
 must await God
   coming at his time
     in his season
     in his way
     to his place.

In our waiting—
 we will often wait alone.
   Others will leave
     will give up
     will be busy about many things.

Being quiet
  is the answer.
        Not silence—
                silence can be empty.
        Not noise—
                noise can be hollow.
                    but...

The active listening—
  of a contemplative heart
        bursting with love
                and expectancy—
                knowing the Master will come
                    sheltering us by day
                    warming us in the night.

Russell Terra

First Week of Advent

Sunday

Seek the Lord and his strength, seek his face continually.   Cf. 1 Chr 16

The Lord is Someone who is to be discovered by us. Someone we should search for and who is always ready to transform our lives the moment we shall encounter him.

God hides so that we may go and seek him, and keep on looking for him until we find him whom our heart and soul desire.

Our life on this earth should be a continual search, a seeking for God so that we may find him, and having found him, keep him ever by our side. For to find God is to keep him, if we really love him.

And lest we should become discouraged by a long and seemingly fruitless search, Sacred Scripture tells us how to go about seeking the Lord in order to find him:

You shall indeed find him when you search after him
with your whole heart and your whole soul.

How do we prepare our heart and soul to seek God? We prepare the day we are determined to keep his commandments, the day we take stock of ourselves and repent, thereby receiving understanding and having our eyes opened to be able to see him whom we hope to find. For unless we become clean of heart we shall not be able to see and discover him.

Before we set off to seek and find him, we have to take stock of ourselves and take a good look at the chamber of our heart to see who is there, what is there taking up the place that rightfully belongs to him. In other words we have to "clean house" and clean up the room we shall bring him into. For to find the Lord is to hold on to him, and bring him inside us so that he may abide in our hearts. For the Lord desires to come and live with us.

If we are not seeking him as we should, it is because there is a dimension missing in our repentance: the realization of what it entailed him in pain and suffering to ransom us from the penalty of our sins. Only when we have experienced the need to be forgiven shall we be truly sorry and turn to the Lord, who is always ready to forgive us. And only then shall we seek and follow after him with all the love of our hearts, because one to whom much has been forgiven loves much in return.

Brother Anthony Opisso

―――――――

Your ways, O Lord, make known to me;
teach me your paths.
Guide me in your truth and teach me,
for you are God my savior. Ps 25

―――――――

If you set out to meet God, he will come to meet you.
Curé of Ars

Monday

Hear the word of the Lord, O nations....
Here is your God...
  he comes to save you. Jer 31; Is 35

God made all things not for themselves, but for a greater creature. When all was ready, he made the king and ruler of this vast universe—he made man. He breathed his divine life into man, made him his child and was most eager to have him share in his own boundless and eternal happiness.

But man spoiled God's plan by disobedience. Still God did not reject him. He made a new and even more wonderful plan—one which in even our wildest dreams we could never have imagined—to bring man to the happiness he had prepared for him. He went, so to speak, to the very limit of even divine wisdom and power and love to show how eager he was to have man be eternally happy. He sent his one and only Son, the Second Person of the Blessed Trinity, to become a member of the human race, to bring man back to God, by having this beloved Son endure the most shameful and painful death on a cross, in order that man might realize the immensity and intensity of his love and his eagerness for man's happiness.

He has given back to us the divine life, made us his children again, members of his Church, and through her given us this very Savior as food and drink to nourish us as children of God. He guides and guards us through all the trials and temptations of life. This is clearly stated by St. John:

God's love was revealed in our midst
  in this way:
he sent his only Son to the world
that we might have life through him.

+ A. A. Noser

Lord, you have loved us first!
We speak of you as if your first love had been only
once,
but instead, your love is continually first, day after
day, eternally.
When I awaken in the morning and raise my spirit
up to you,
you are the first to love me first.
When I arise at dawn and lift up my spirit and my
prayer,
you are there before me, you have already loved me
first.
It is always so.
We ungratefully speak as if your first love had been
only once,
while you, you alone, are the mercy which is never
failing. Sören Kierkegaard

Charity is responding to God's love and drawing upon it to spread the same thing to other people.

Hubert van Zeller

Tuesday

Justice shall flower in his days,
and profound peace.... Ps 72

Inner peace! A man who is at peace with God radiates peaceful living in his daily duties. It is not possible to enjoy peace when the soul is warring against its Creator. There is no peace in the gauntlet of sin marked with signs: "pleasure," "escape," "fun"—nothing genuine here.

Every sin is a discordant note. What folly in the external, unwise pursuits of peace that are outside God's laws and do not recognize his primacy!

Troubled men, unsettled human beings, disordered mankind can find only one way back to peace. It is God's way.

A life ordered on prayer and spiritual vitality, concerned with the things of God, must be a life of deep, deep peace. It is not reserved for cloistered religious. It is for all men. The clamor of the city, the hustle of a work day—nothing can disturb or uproot the genuine peace of a man immersed in, concerned with, thoughtful of, and practicing always the love of God.   *Don Costello*

———

Lord, make me an instrument of your peace.
Where there is hatred, let me sow love;
where there is injury, pardon;
where there is doubt, faith;
where there is despair, hope;
where there is darkness, light;
and where there is sadness, joy.
O Divine Master, grant that I may not so much seek
to be consoled as to console;
to be understood as to understand;
to be loved as to love;
for it is in giving that we receive;
it is in pardoning that we are pardoned;
and it is in dying that we are born to eternal life.
St. Francis of Assisi

———

In his will is our peace.   *Dante*

Wednesday

I shall dwell in the house of the Lord
for years to come. Ps 23:6

When a very dear friend visits us, we do not let him sit alone for hours in our house without having a word with him. God is surely much more than even our very dearest friend on earth. We should remember that God is living with and in us at all times, at every moment of the day and night, and so we should often enter into conversation with him. We should try to speak to him with the simplicity and filial trust of a little child to its father. In this way we grow in a living faith in his presence within our heart, and turning to him, we often enter this temple, until it gradually becomes a habit with us to live with him there, so that we are "on fire with the Holy Spirit."

+ A. A. Noser

Burn within me, O Holy Fire,
so that,
chaste in body and pure of heart,
I may deserve to see God.   Brian Moore, S.J.

God is not wont to speak to a soul that does not speak to him.   *St. Alphonsus de Liguori*

Thursday

Let our lives be honest and holy in this present age,
as we wait for the happiness to come when our great
God reveals himself in glory. Ti 2

Why are we almost afraid to use the expression "holy"? Perhaps our fear comes from its misuse in such derogatory remarks as a "holy Joe" or "holier than thou."

We ought to get accustomed to making the whole concept of holiness, holy people and holy things a most pleasing and familiar reference. How frequently God himself takes to his name the word holy—Holy Trinity; Holy, Holy, Holy, Lord God of Hosts, and so on!

What really is holiness? Who is holy? Where can holiness be found? If it is all bound up in the will of God, then it is simple. A mother who fulfills her duty by feeding her baby is doing something holy. A secretary typing diligently is indeed performing a holy act. Of course, we are supposing that all interior dispositions are proper, with the will and the heart in tune with God.

Holiness as a constant state is a state of beatitude, of happiness. St. Francis of Assisi amid all his poverty radiated happiness. His material condition was irrelevant.

And so in striving for holiness we have set in motion...gladness! All the prayer, sacrifice and energy we pour out to do God's will is what life's purpose is all about—*holiness!*   *Don Costello*

―――――――

Breathe in me, O Holy Spirit,
that my thoughts may all be holy.
Act in me, O Holy Spirit,
that my work, too, may be holy.
Draw my heart, O Holy Spirit,
that I may love only what is holy.
Strengthen me, O Holy Spirit,
that I may defend all that is holy.
Guard me, O Holy Spirit,
that I myself may always be holy.   St. Augustine

―――――――

Holiness does not consist in doing extraordinary things, but rather in doing ordinary things in an extraordinary way.   *Cardinal H. E. Manning*

Friday

The Lord is my light and my salvation.   Ps 27

Consider that your God loves you more than you can possibly love him. What do you fear? David found comfort in these words: *The Lord thinks of me.* Then you should say to him: Into your arms I cast myself, O my God. I want to think of nothing but of loving you. I am ready to do whatever you ask of me. Not only do you desire my well-being, you are concerned about it. Therefore, I leave to you the care of my salvation. In you is my rest, and it will always be in you, since you will that I place all my hope in you. *"As soon as I lie down, I fall peacefully asleep, for you alone, O Lord, bring security to my dwelling."*

"Think of the Lord in goodness." These words encourage us to have greater confidence in the divine mercy than fear of the divine justice, since God is far more inclined to do good than to punish. So says St. James: *"Mercy triumphs over judgment."* Hence the Apostle St. Peter warns us that in the fears we feel for our concerns, whether they are temporal or eternal, we must abandon ourselves entirely to the good God who has our salvation so much at heart: *"Cast all your anxiety upon him, because he cares for you."*

In this same regard how beautiful is the title which David gives the Lord when he says that our God is the God who seeks to save: *"God is a saving God for us."* This means, that God does not condemn, but saves everyone; for even though he threatens with his disapproval those who despise him, his mercy is assured to those who fear him, as our Blessed Mother sang in her *Magnificat: "And his mercy is on those who fear him."*

I set these scriptural texts before you, in order that, when you are troubled as to whether you will be saved or lost, you may relieve your mind by considering the desire God has to save you, as is proved by his promises, if only you stand firm in your resolution to serve and love him as he requires.   *St. Alphonsus de Liguori*

O Lord! Every day is for me a new and
*   sweeter call to your inexhaustible love,*
your ineffable mercy!
I wish to give testimony of this to all.
I desire to tell everyone
that you are eternal and providential patience for my
*   soul!*   John Henry Newman

The whole point of mercy is that it goes beyond reason. If God acted on reason alone we would never get to heaven.   *Hubert van Zeller*

Saturday

O Lord of hosts, restore us;
*   if your face shine upon us then we shall be safe.*
                    Ps 80

If anything is clear, it is that Christ by his coming among us and his willing to be one with us has ennobled our human nature. He did this by joining our weakness to the strength of his Godhead in the unity of the one Person, the Son of God. This it is that should make us lift up our heads when the weight of our misery would press us down. More than anything, the world needs today a shortage of long faces; and Christians who realize how high Christ has elevated our poor nature should refuse to contribute a single pinch of pessimism to the sum total there is in the world.

It is the part of wisdom not to undervalue or neglect God's strength and power in Christ when we feel abandoned to human helplessness in our battles with pain. In fact, when we are being crowded by misery, let us go early and seek the aid of Christ's sacred humanity, where there is true healing. St. Paul writes: *God was pleased to have all fullness abide in him [Christ]...in him all things hold together.*

Money will take you anywhere you want to go—except to heaven, and buy you anything you want to have—except happiness. But you don't need money to appeal to the power of Christ to help you in distress.

The S.O.S. you send him in prayer, the prayer of faith, will rescue you from despondency. It will greatly contribute to elevate your spirit. And any doctor will tell you that an elevation of spirit, a cheerful and hopeful outlook, helps immensely in combatting the doldrums that especially plague those suffering from a continuing illness.

Victor L. Dux

———

Lord, deliver me from the tormenting temptation of looking upon illness as a useless part of life, as a failure of my existence, a period empty and without value.

May I accept the cross of illness, Lord, knowing that in your eyes nothing is lost. Reveal to me, O Lord, the meaning of my suffering.

Never permit me to feel sorry for myself or have excessive fear of what may happen to me. Only thus will I be able to look to you with confidence and contribute to the serenity of those around me.

V. Del Mazza, S.D.B.

The problem of evil is to a large extent the problem of pain. To those who apply the solution of faith there is no problem at all. *Hubert van Zeller*

Second Week of Advent

Sunday

Behold the joy that comes to you from God.   Bar 4

True joy, like true peace, is something of which the world has no conception. True joy is a foretaste of the bliss of heaven and is not the kind of which the senses tire. But since the experience of it is necessarily rare, and is indeed a special grace, the senses are hardly given time to tire of it.

If the soul can be brought to see that the only lasting joy is joy in Christ, then no temporal misfortune can come in to spoil it. *Sorrowful yet always rejoicing...we seem to have nothing yet everything is ours.*

Christ's peace is a quality which no man can take from us. The joy which comes from the same source is equally secure. So the joy which all too easily can be taken from us—by people, circumstances, adversity, and above all by our own moods—must be raised to the level of love and directed by the light of grace.

True joy not only has its source in true love and finds its object in true love but achieves its temporal fulfillment in the exercise of true love. Love is not only the fulfillment of the law but also the fulfillment of joy.

Hubert van Zeller

O Mary, who abandoned your soul to happiness by offering it to God, grant that in our gift to God our joy may be complete.

O Virgin radiant with joy, grant that we may believe in the happiness which God in his love wills to offer us;

Make joy bloom again in hearts given over to sadness;

Teach us to detach ourselves from worldly pleasures and to seek our happiness in God;

Help us to radiate the witness of Christian joy;

Through your presence in our life, be for us the font of a joy which is ever new.   Jean Galot

The mysterious thing about joy is not that it can pierce a suffering but that it can remain with it and survive it.   Hubert van Zeller

Monday

Show us, O Lord, your kindness,
  and grant us your salvation. Ps 85

God is always faithful in his mercy. Certainly he does not deprive man of his existential and historical drama, but he lives it with him. For all time the Lord has made his dwelling among men to remain always with us. As the waters of the sea wash against the rock, so are we ceaselessly followed and accompanied by the loving fidelity of God. For the thousands and thousands of generations since time began, this merciful love has been bestowed on man in kindness and faithfulness.

The holy fidelity of God persists in following us despite all our infidelities. Just as a light does not cease to shine upon a closed door, so does heavenly mercy never cease to accompany us in order to save us. Even if we should lose confidence in the Lord, he will continue to have confidence and hope in us. And only if the Lord would cease to be infinitely good and merciful, and we should become totally and infinitely evil and unfaithful—both metaphysical impossibilities—until such a time there will always be for us the possibility of salvation and of rebirth.   *V. Del Mazza, S.D.B.*

I will hear what God proclaims:
    The Lord—for he proclaims peace
To his people, and to his faithful ones,
    and to those who put in him their hope.
Near indeed is his salvation to those who fear him,
    glory dwelling in our land.
Kindness and truth shall meet;
    justice and peace shall kiss.
Truth shall spring out of the earth,
    and justice shall look down from heaven.
The Lord himself will give his benefits;
    our land shall yield its increase.
Justice shall walk before him,
    and salvation, along the way of his steps.

                                                        Ps 85

If I but once lose the sense of God's mercy I lose the only support of which I can be infallibly certain.

                                        Hubert van Zeller

Tuesday

*Here comes with power
     the Lord God....
Like a shepherd he feeds his flock....*   Is 40

No earthly images can come up to the truth that God became the Son of Man—that the Word became flesh, and was born of woman. This ineffable mystery surpasses human words. No titles of earth can Christ give to himself, ever so lowly or mean, which will fitly show us his condescension. His act and deed is too great even for his own lips to utter it. Yet he delights in the image of the Good Shepherd, as conveying to us, in such degree as we can receive it, some notion of the degradation, hardship and pain, which he underwent for our sake.
Cardinal Newman

———————

*The Lord is my shepherd; I shall not want.
     In verdant pastures he gives me repose;
Beside restful waters he leads me;
     he refreshes my soul.
He guides me in right paths
     for his name's sake.
Even though I walk in the dark valley
     I fear no evil; for you are at my side
With your rod and your staff
     that give me courage.
You spread the table before me
     in the sight of my foes;
You anoint my head with oil;
     my cup overflows.
Only goodness and kindness follow me
     all the days of my life;
And I shall dwell in the house of the Lord
     for years to come.*   Ps 23

The Lord is my Shepherd. Lead me forth. Hear me, O Thou Shepherd of Israel. Gently lead me.

Cardinal Newman

Wednesday

They that hope in the Lord will renew their strength,
they will soar as with eagles' wings. Is 40

If today our humanity is groaning and quivering like a machine with its internal mechanism broken, the chief reason is the absence of theological hope. Instead of placing confidence in God, as in past centuries, man today is depending on social programming and electronic computers. This attitude provides an ever more extensive field for development of interior crises. Without doubt, an existence bracketed between two zeroes—the zero of birth and the zero of death—cannot fail to produce undulations in one's spiritual life: agitations, frustrations. We have learned that not a few of our social disturbances, our numerous exhibitions of impatience against someone or something, are in great part the effect of the theological impoverishment of our spiritual horizons.

For the Christian, to hope is to give value and poetry to our history, made up as it is of miseries, failures, mourning and contradictions; to hope means to see and enjoy the divine light which radiates from the city of God, surmounting and beautifying every cloud and every tempest. In this sense every Christian could be compared to a swimmer who, defending himself from the violence of the waves, lets these very waves carry him to shore.

V. Del Mazza, S.D.B.

*Lord, I want to be among those who risk their
    lives for you.*
*What good is a road, if at the end of it there is
    not someone I love,*
someone waiting for me?

*Lord, let me walk toward the good, toward
    the worthwhile, toward you.*
I want to spend my life proclaiming your Word.

*You have often told me to have confidence in you,
to entrust myself to you, to your power:
    merciful, provident, wondrous.*

*Lord, fill me with your love.
Make me ready for your stupendous, divine
    adventure,
which consists in living with you, for you,
to your glory, unto death and for all eternity.
    Amen.*
                                    V. Del Mazza, S.D.B.

God has assured us of the security that awaits us.
Hope is taking him at his word.   *Hubert van Zeller*

Thursday

*The Lord is good to all
    and compassionate toward all his works.*

                                    Ps 145

Pardon is love in its highest and noblest expression.
Perfect pardon can come solely from one who is utterly
innocent, that is, from one who cannot harm and therefore cannot have need of the pardon of others. Only in

God is this possible. Each one of us has need of being pardoned by our neighbor for something or other: often enough our pardon is rather justice. Only the Lord, by nature, can gratuitously pardon.

Still more. When God pardons us he produces innocence in our soul: it is like a new creation, a real rehabilitation.   *V. Del Mazza, S.D.B.*

━━━━━━

You, O most sweet Lord, are bountiful to me above all merit, and more than I would dare hope or ask for.

Although I am unworthy of every good, yet your greatness and infinite goodness never cease to bless even the ungrateful and those who have withdrawn from you.

Oh, convert us to you, so that we may be thankful, humble, and devout, because you are our salvation.   Thomas à Kempis

━━━━━━

No matter how many sins, even serious ones, and imperfections a person may have committed, he must never despair of salvation, nor lose confidence in God. The divine mercy is infinitely greater than human malice.
                                    St. John Chrysostom

Friday

I, the Lord, your God,
    teach you what is for your good,
    and lead you on the way you should go.   Is 48

Christ:

Walk before me in truth and seek me always in the simplicity of your heart.

Whoever walks before me in the truth shall be defended from the assaults of evil, and the truth will deliver him from deceivers and from the detractions of the wicked.

I who am the truth will teach you those things which are right and pleasing in my sight.

Disciple:

Lord, this is true; let it be done unto me as you say, I beseech you. Let your truth teach me, guard me and keep me till I arrive at my salvation.   *Thomas à Kempis*

When love calls me, I do not ask questions: I follow.
Donoso Cortés

Saturday

Give us new life, and we will call upon your name.
Ps 80

Mankind has always loved the light and dreaded darkness, whether one thinks of the physical or spiritual order, whether it is the light and darkness of the world outside ourselves, or the light and darkness of the mind and soul within.

We will welcome at Christmas him who is the Light of the world. Following him we shall not walk in darkness.

The darkness which results from and accompanies a sinful life is difficult to penetrate, even for the rays of divine Light. A curtain has been drawn between the soul and God; grace has been expelled; the eyes of the mind and heart have been turned away; the voice of conscience has been stifled and stilled.

But the mercy and goodness of God know no limits. The prayers of the blind in the Gospel are still effective today: *Lord, that our eyes be opened; Lord, that I may see.* For he came not only to give light, but that they may have life.   *+ Robert F. Joyce*

―――――――――――

Incline my heart to your decrees and not to gain.
Turn away my eyes from seeing what is vain;
  by your way give me life. Ps 119

―――――――――――

Grace should be the moving force of all that the Christian does. He lives, works, loves by it. He shapes his opinions by it, practices virtue on the strength of it, prays by the light of it. Not for a moment can he do without it.

Hubert van Zeller

Third Week of Advent

Sunday

(For December 17 to December 24, see pages 46 – 56.)

*Rejoice in the Lord always; again I say rejoice! The
Lord is near.*   Phil 4

We rejoice in wonder as we reflect on the mystery of
God having become man to show us the unspeakable
riches of his goodness, and beauty, and compassionate
love. We wonder, and through his gift of grace, we rejoice
and are moved to share our joy with everyone because we
realize that what we have seen in faith and what has been
given to us is not for ourselves alone, but to be shared
with all, since it is a gift of the merciful love of God for us.

At Christmas we do want to share what we have and
especially what we are. In this way we show that we are
children of our Heavenly Father who shares himself and
his own Son with us so that through him we may share in
his life and have his peace and his joy.

Our desire to share comes from the love that gives us
life, the creative love of God which brought us into being
and which he shares with us. Because it is from this love,
it is outgoing—it reaches out to others, it takes us out of
ourselves and even leads us to forget ourselves and our
personal concerns so that we may be absorbed in the
personal needs of others. We are moved to give what we
have and what we are in the service of others no matter
who they are because of our love for them.

The quality of our service to them is measured by the quality of our love. That is why it is not what our gift looks like that really counts for us and for them but rather the looks of our inner heart that make the gift of service pleasing and acceptable to those who receive it.

Moreover, this loving service is always healing since it comes through us from the source of all love who is God. We believe that Jesus came to give his life for us that we might have his life and his joy. No greater service could be given to us with greater love than this.

To share the joy and peace of Christmas we must share in the spirit of Jesus. We must have his values. We must love with his love and think with his thoughts.

There is a deep mystery in this but it brings the light of God to our life. To live by his light is to live in peace and joy, humbly resting securely in the hand of our loving Heavenly Father. In this love we will live in simplicity, trusting the divine Goodness to provide for our needs in due time through our suitable effort, and we will share with others all we are and all we have in the spirit of Christmas to bring the joy and peace of Christ to all we can reach.   *Humberto Cardinal Medeiros*

Sing joyfully to the Lord, all you lands;
serve the Lord with gladness;
come before him with joyful song.
Know that the Lord is God;
he made us, his we are;
his people, the flock he tends.
Enter his gates with thanksgiving,
his courts with praise;
Give thanks to him; bless his name, for he is good:
the Lord, whose kindness endures forever,
and his faithfulness, to all generations.

Ps 100

Joy is life's tree—grief but its leaf.   *Abram Ryan*

Monday

(For December 17 to December 24, see pages 46 – 56.)

Your ways, O Lord, make known to me;
teach me your paths,
Guide me in your truth and teach me,
for you are God my savior. Ps 25

The heart and source of our Christian life is the Gospel. It is a matter of simple logic. If God appeared as man on earth to show us how to love and live, there is only one important thing to do, love and live as we find the God-man doing. The primary source for this information is the Gospel. It is here we see the God-man in action.

Vatican II "urges all the Christian faithful to learn by frequent reading of the divine Scriptures the 'excelling knowledge of Jesus Christ' (Phil 3:8)...." To be in step with the Church I must read the Scriptures. Not just sporadically, but regularly.

More than that. If this is the word of God, then I must approach it prayerfully, meditatively. If this is the word of God, then certainly it is one way in which he wants to communicate with me. I have to be open and receptive to any inspiration that may come along. I have to let it speak to me. I have to listen so I can get the message without gloss, without mitigating its demands. This means I have to go back to the Scriptures again and again. Then, hopefully, my judgments, my attitudes, my conduct will be molded and guided by the spirit of the Gospel.

If I expose myself often enough to the example of Christ who came not to be served but to serve, maybe I will begin to serve by a spontaneous giving of self. In my own way I can bring the Gospel to bear on the circle in which I move. It may not be world-shaking. It may be just a casual encounter of someone in need, a phone call, a visit to a hospital. It may be on a bus, in the elevator, in the office, at home; it may be a warm greeting, a handclasp, a smile. These fall into the same category as the cup of cold water mentioned in the Gospel. Or it may be the rugged fight for fair housing or the effective end of racial discrimination. Whatever it may be, it will represent an effort to relate my daily life to the spirit of the Gospel.

Albert J. Nimeth

━━━━━━━━━

Father, your Son, the Lord Jesus Christ, was salt and light here on earth. Help us to walk in his way by serving the needs of others so that we too may be salt and light for the world.

━━━━━━━━━

"I am the way, and the truth, and the life;
no one comes to the Father but through me.
If you really knew me, you would know my
Father also." *Jn 14*

Tuesday

(For December 17 to December 24, see pages 46 – 56.)

*The Lord is close to the brokenhearted;
and those who are crushed in spirit he saves.*

Ps 34

Too many of us confuse the whole idea of compassion with a feeling. Compassion is a real understanding of our neighbor's affliction and the will to help. We may feel cold and unmoved by the sight, but we know by our reason that a derelict fallen in the street, bleeding and unconscious, needs help. The Samaritan who had compassion on the man beaten by robbers might have *felt* it was a thankless task, but his act of compassion was strong-willed and determined.

Emotions and feelings may accompany an act of compassion, just as we sometimes compassionate the sorrowful and suffering with our tears. But these aren't necessary. To live by compassion is to be alert to the needs of others. It can be a real deed of compassion when a parent gives up a night's sleep to sit by a feverish child.

To live by compassion may be even heroic. In the act of redemption, Christ's 'compassion for wandering, strayed, lost, bewildered lambs and sheep demonstrates the supreme act of compassion—the compassion of God for humankind.

When thoughts of compassion come to mind and there is a reasonable occasion to act, let us transform the troubles of others into the compassionate wine of God's joy.   *Don Costello*

O My God—
  Teach me to be generous,
  To serve you as you deserve to be served,
  To give without counting the cost,
  To fight without fear of being wounded,
  To work without seeking rest, and
  To spend myself without expecting any reward
    but the knowledge that I am doing your
    holy will.   Traditional

Be compassionate, as your Father is compassionate.

Lk 6:36

Wednesday

(For December 17 to December 24, see pages 46 – 56.)

Kindness and truth shall meet;
justice and peace shall kiss.
Truth shall spring out of the earth,
and justice shall look down from heaven.

Ps 85

Imagine a world of untruth: no one believable; no person's word trustworthy; honesty just a myth.... The whole fabric of civilization is intertwined with the vital fibers of truth. Pull out truth, and what is left?

And the truth which is eternal, unchanging, is in the word of God. His word to us speaks volumes in one sentence. His truth echoes everlastingly in a single promise. If the promise of gold could drive prospectors far and wide, what should the promise of eternal happiness motivate us to do, knowing full well that what the Lord says is absolute truth? There's no question about it. It is true.

The habit of truthfulness should be developed over a lifetime so that, in a moment of temptation, almost instinctively, one tells the truth.

Truth does make you free, as Scripture says. There is that bird-soaring freedom in knowing that we are not bogged down by our own deceits.

Living in truth, swimming in truth, flying high in a buoyancy that is once again the joy of God living truth, a human being comes to experience an exhilaration, vibrantly in him.   *Don Costello*

Heavenly Father,
to you every heart lies open,
every will speaks,
nothing is hidden.
By the in-pouring of the Holy Spirit
purify the thoughts of my heart,
that I may love you perfectly,
and praise you worthily.
Through Christ our Lord.   Traditional

The search for truth is the search for God. To search for truth without God, or for God without truth: which is more absurd?   *Hubert van Zeller*

Thursday

(For December 17 to December 24, see pages 46 – 56.)

My love shall never leave you
    nor my covenant of peace be shaken,
        says the Lord, who has mercy on you. Is 54

Loneliness, a feeling of abandonment, is surely one of the more painful of human difficulties. This isolating smog frequently settles upon the old, but it can choke the joy of life in the young also, and even in those who seem surrounded with friends and compatible companions.

A person's spirit has its place of deep withdrawal, where others cannot follow, and where, if it does not find

God present in some manner, it experiences the chill of naked aloneness, of unfulfilled needs. This pain can come upon the rich as well as the most needy, on the famous as well as the forgotten, on the sanguine and the extrovert as well as the melancholy and the introvert.

The soul is an empty mold needing to be filled; a parched desert soil needing to be watered and wakened to life; a vacuum tense with the need of an equalizing, tranquilizing presence.

We should find relief from aching loneliness in the comforting words of the Scriptures. If I feel ignored, unappreciated, abandoned, or completely insignificant in the crowded, busy world, I can know from his word that God's fatherly love embraces me.

> As a father has compassion on his children,
>   so the Lord has compassion on those who fear
>   him.
> Merciful and gracious is the Lord,
>   slow to anger and abounding in kindness....
> Not according to our sins does he deal with us,
>   nor does he requite us according to our crimes.

His love for me is like the love of a mother for her child—no, it *exceeds* it.

> But Zion said, "The Lord has forsaken me;
>   my Lord has forgotten me."
> Can a mother forget her infant,
>   be without tenderness for the child of her
>   womb?
> Even should she forget,
>   I will never forget you.

Anthony J. Pfarr, S.J.

> O God, you are my God whom I seek;
>   for you my flesh pines and my soul thirsts

like the earth, parched, lifeless and without
    water.
You are my help,
    and in the shadow of your wings
    I shout for joy.
My soul clings fast to you;
    your right hand upholds me.   Ps 63

———————

Seek what you seek, but not where you seek it. Your heart has been made for God and it shall be restless until it rests in him.   *St. Augustine*

Friday

(For December 17 to December 24, see pages 46 – 56.)

Thus says the Lord:
Observe what is right, do what is just;
    for my salvation is about to come,
    my justice, about to be revealed. Is 56

We have to center our life around something which determines our mode of thought, speech and action. This is sometimes called motivation, or standards, or ideals, or purposes, and it largely determines our mode of life.

We may be egocentric, making the world revolve around ourselves on the principle that we are the center of the universe, sufficient unto ourselves, with all things required to promote our personal satisfactions and interests. This is the great temptation for all human beings, the instinct of self-preservation becoming exaggerated.

Or we may make mankind the central object of creation, an end in itself. The current theories of our day have glorified man, indeed deified him, as if he created himself, sustained himself in being, and was the only end and purpose of creation.

Finally we may have a God-centered world, in which we acknowledge the Creator as the source of all life, as the Author of our being, as the ultimate Legislator of all law. Here is wisdom, because only God is eternal, is unchangeable, and is the only fount from which life can have meaning.

Indeed we have to be in some degree egocentric, since we have responsibility for the life and talents given us, but we are not independent, and we have no guarantee of our life's span. And likewise we have to serve mankind by virtue of Christ's command, our natural love of each other, and dependence on each other, but not as if mankind were the ultimate and final goal of all creation.

We learn that to have a God-centered world we must have regard for divine and natural law, and for the place of man in God's Providence. We begin to understand why we must love ourselves and our fellow men, because we share in God's life and God's plan. Our talents, our goods, our time, our service, our love, are largely sterile if they have not the seal of divinity in them. Men are often far from lovable and admirable in themselves, but they command love and respect as creatures bearing God's image and likeness, as beneficiaries of Christ's Redemption.

Ultimately life has no meaning unless it is centered around God, its source and its end. Any other road, any other approach or attitude is not the way for men that they may have life.   + *Robert F. Joyce*

O merciful Lord, you are never weary of speaking to my poor heart; grant me grace that, if today I hear your voice, my heart may not be hardened.

Cardinal Merry del Val

Worldliness is an attitude of mind before it is a norm of conduct. If I get my mind set towards God, I shall know how to handle that aspect of the world which draws me away from God.　　　　　　　*Hubert van Zeller*

December 17

O Wisdom, you came forth from the mouth of the Most High, and reaching from beginning to end, you ordered all things mightily and sweetly. Come and teach us the way of prudence!

Ancient antiphon

Jesus is Wisdom, the Word, Person equal to the Father. *The word became flesh....* "Out of the mouth of the Most High"—perfect expression of the infinite knowing of God.

"Reaching from end to end...." All the good, beauty, order in the universe, "from end to end," is the work of Wisdom, the Word, together with the Father and the Holy Spirit. *Through him all things came into being....*

"Come and teach us the way of prudence." *Come!* One syllable sums up the advent liturgy, explodes with all the desires built up through centuries in a suffering humanity made for God but alienated from him.

Anthony J. Pfarr, S.J.

O Wisdom...

How our human nature needs the revelation of divine truth and knowledge of the divine moral law, our unaided reason and intelligence proving so inadequate!... How little we see through a glass darkly, how easy to sway our unguided conscience, how tempting to cast aside all restraining truths and commandments for the freedom to think and do as we please!

This is why God has made known his divine truth both by revelation and reason; this is why the Son of God became man and taught by example and word.

+ *Robert F. Joyce*

———————

God of my fathers, Lord of mercy,
    you who have made all things by your word
And in your wisdom have established man
    to rule the creatures produced by you,
To govern the world in holiness and justice,
    and to render judgment in integrity of heart:
Give me Wisdom, the attendant at your
      throne.... Wis 9

———————

The first task of anyone who aspires to wisdom is the consideration of what he himself is.   *John of Salisbury*

December 18

O Adonai and Ruler of the house of Israel, you appeared to Moses in the fire of the burning bush, and on Mount Sinai gave him your law. Come, and with an outstretched arm redeem us!

Ancient antiphon

"O Adonai"—Lord of lords. "Ruler"—a true leader, knowing the way, never swerving from it through personal passion or weakness. Who "appeared to Moses," to the accompaniment of thunder: come now as a man of meekness and peace, even as a small child.

"With an outstretched arm redeem us!" Those short baby arms stretched out for Mary's care—they shall redeem us in the strength of God. Moses saved his people in battle by pleading to God with outstretched arms sustained by those of his captains; this child shall save with arms stretched out upon a cross, sustained by nails—rather, by love. *Anthony J. Pfarr, S.J.*

———————

You gave him your law...

There are those who prefer to act on impulse and feeling, meeting each problem as seems expedient, having no guidelines by which to measure.

It does not seem to occur to them how contrary this is to the teaching of Christ, who required belief, who insisted on the commandments, who sent apostles to teach, who required obedience and gave it.

Indeed he taught love and practiced it, but he knew human nature, and knew that love alone does not overcome our selfishness, our laziness, our appetites, our greed, our indifference, our ingratitude to God and men. He knew, with his infinite wisdom, that men needed laws and creed, and fidelity to them, that they may have life. *+ Robert F. Joyce*

———————

Be good to your servant, that I may live
and keep your words.
Open my eyes, that I may consider
the wonders of your law. Ps 119

———————

God's precepts are heavy to the fearful, light to the loving. *St. Thomas Aquinas*

December 19

O Root of Jesse, you stand as an ensign for mankind;
before you kings shall keep silence, and to you all
nations shall have recourse. Come, save us, and do
not delay.   Ancient antiphon

David, son of Jesse, was a great king, but only a figure
of the King who was to be the perfect flowering of that
kingly line. A perfect flower has sprung up from poor
humanity rooted in the dung heap of sin. Come! Do not
delay!   *Anthony J. Pfarr, S.J.*

To you all shall have recourse.
    A shoot shall sprout from the stump of Jesse,
    and from his roots a bud shall blossom....
Not by appearance shall he judge,
    nor my hearsay shall he decide,
But he shall judge the poor with justice,
    and decide aright for the land's afflicted. Is 11

O God, with your judgment endow the king,
    and with your justice, the king's son....
He shall have pity for the lowly and the poor;
    the lives of the poor he shall save. Ps 72

One cannot love without serving.   *Hubert van Zeller*

December 20

O Key of David and Scepter of the house of Israel:
you open and no one closes; you close and no one

opens. Come and deliver us from the chains of prison—we who sit in darkness and in the shadow of death.   Ancient antiphon

The Ruling power shall be his. *The Lord God will give to him the throne of David his father.* "Key of David"—He alone can make man free. He was sent to *proclaim liberty to captives....*   Anthony J. Pfarr, S.J.

―――――――――

Come and deliver us...

It is wonderful to notice in the prophecies of the Old Testament how they settle down more and more upon the House of David....

The genealogy of our Lord from David, in that imperfect-perfect manner recognized by the Jews, has been preserved to us. When we look at the line we are struck by many things. David himself was a great saint, but also a great sinner, and our Lord came from that union which had followed on David's great sin. We can follow down the line of his ancestors and notice that though our Lord provided for himself a spotless Mother, he by no means provided spotless forefathers. In this, as in many other ways, *he became like mankind;* though in him sin was not, yet so closely did he allow himself to be allied to it....

This is to look at life along the plane of God. From the next world how differently will perspectives appear! *The base things of the world, and the things that are contemptible, has God chosen, and things that are not, that he may bring to nought things that are: that no flesh should glory in his sight.*
                              + Alban Goodier

―――――――――

Lord, you are love.
Give me the grace to believe in your love,
*   to be a joy-filled apostle of your infinite mercy.*

O Holy Spirit, enlighten and convert my heart,
  invade my soul,
that my life may be one with my wounded brethren
  whom I meet on the way,
and that I may be hope for those who offend your
  merciful love.   V. Del Mazza, S.D.B.

━━━━━━━━━━

Nothing graces the Christian soul so greatly as mercy.
St. Ambrose

December 21

O Rising Dawn, radiance of the light eternal and
sun of justice; come and enlighten those who sit in
darkness and in the shadow of death.

Ancient antiphon

The darkness of centuries begins to lift, the soft light
of dawn breaks over Bethlehem's hills. Soon the full
brightness of the eternal light, of the Sun of Justice, shall
shine upon the whole world. So long, so very long, have
men sat in darkness, in the shadow of death. We must
accept the light individually, for some show by evil deeds
and toleration of injustice that they prefer darkness.

Anthony J. Pfarr, S.J.

━━━━━━━━━━

Come and Shine...

Blessed be the Lord, the God of Israel
  because he has visited and ransomed his people.
He has raised a horn of saving strength for us
  in the house of David his servant,
As he promised through the mouths of his holy ones,
  the prophets of ancient times:

Salvation from our enemies
    and from the hands of all our foes....
    He, the Dayspring, shall visit us in his mercy
To shine on those who sit in darkness
    and in the shadow of death,
    to guide our feet into the way of peace.   *Lk 1*

━━━━━━━━━━

*Let me beg of Thee to lead me on in Thy perfect
and narrow way, and to be a lantern to my feet, and
a light to my path, while I walk in it.*

*What is it to me how my future path lies, if it be
but Thy path? What is it to me whither it leads, as
long as in the end it leads to Thee? What is it to me
what terror befalls me, if Thou be but at hand to
protect and strengthen me?*

*Thou has brought me thus far in order to bring
me further, in order to bring me on to the end. Thou
wilt never leave me nor forsake me.*

Cardinal Newman

━━━━━━━━━━

The Lord is God, and he has given us light.

Ps 118

December 22

*O King of the gentiles and the Desired of all, you are
the cornerstone that binds two into one. Come and
save poor man whom you fashioned out of clay.*

Ancient antiphon

Cornerstone uniting side and side, foundation and structure, in the temple of God; uniting Jew and pagan, the two great divisions in the mind of the Jewish theocracy. All who are to be part of the city of God are united and built upon Christ. *See, I am laying a cornerstone in Zion, an approved stone, and precious.*

All are "fashioned out of clay," and no brick or tile is chosen because of its inherent worth. The choosing is a free gift of God, and we must give ourselves to the building up of his Church.   *Anthony J. Pfarr, S.J.*

The Desired of all...

It is not mere fancy of historians which sees in the history of almost, if not quite all, ancient peoples a certain looking into the future, a certain consciousness of undevelopment among themselves, a certain craving for something which they did not yet have, but which was yet to come to them—a light and more perfect understanding, a power for good, a completion and satisfaction in their own being which would bring them peace and contentment....

The satisfaction of this hungering, expressed in many ways, is not the least of the beauties of the Old Testament, and finds its echo in the New.   *+. Alban Goodier*

Thou who art all purity came to an impure race to raise them to Thy purity. Thou, the brightness of God's glory, didst come in a body of flesh, which was pure and holy as Thyself, not having spot or wrinkle or any such thing but that it should be holy and without blemish; *and this Thou didst for our sake, that we might be partakers of Thy holiness.*   Cardinal Newman

Form all together one choir, so that...you may sing
with one voice to the Father through Jesus Christ.

St. Ignatius of Antioch

December 23

O Emmanuel, our King and Lawgiver, the Expected
of nations and their Savior: Come to save us, O Lord
our God!   Ancient antiphon

What a meaningful list of names for us to dwell on:
Emmanuel, King, Lawgiver, Savior, Lord, God.

"Emmanuel—God with us." What precious intimacies
does this name recall, in the sacrifice and sacrament, in
his Mystical Body, in the divine indwelling.

Come, Lord Jesus!   *Anthony J. Pfarr, S.J.*

Come...O Lord our God!

Had we lived in the time of Christ, would we have
been on hand to welcome the newborn King? Would we
have been fortunate enough to hear the good news of
great joy? And if we had heard it, would we have done
anything about it?... It is quite possible we would have
been creatures of our times, chained to our beds, our
comfort, our unbelief. It would have been a Christmas
without Christ.

We, however, have been born in an age of faith, weak
though it may be. We are the fortunate heirs of the de-
voted ages of faith. Ours is the heritage of believers and
that is why we can make the transition from Bethlehem to
the tabernacle without strain. We can experience the wonderful traditions of Christmas carried on in the Eucharist.
It is our task then to pass on these traditions, fortified and

purified, so that every generation after us will know the joy of the good news, Emmanuel, God-with-us!

Albert J. Nimeth

O come, O come, Emmanuel,
And ransom captive Israel,
That mourns in lonely exile here,
Until the Son of God appear.
     Rejoice! Rejoice! Emmanuel
     Shall come to thee, O Israel.

Traditional advent hymn

I behold a mystery strange and wondrous. The cave is heaven, the Virgin is the throne of the cherubim, the manger is the place where the Incomprehensible is laid, Christ our God.   *Byzantine Liturgy*

December 24

The Word became flesh
and made his dwelling among us.... Jn 1

As we reflect on the first Christmas night, we recall the simplicity and the mystery of the occasion. It was a time when our God and Savior came to earth. It was the end of our aloneness and the beginning of God-with-us. Christ left the tabernacle of his mother's womb because *"his delight was to be with the children of men."* This very same thing happens every day on our altars. Day after day Christ returns to take his place among us. He leaves the tabernacle of heaven to come to earth and then he leaves the tabernacle of the altar to come to our hearts. Every union with Christ is Christmas all over again.

Albert J. Nimeth

Bethlehem hath opened Eden,
  Come! Let us behold:
Sweetness we have found once hidden,
  Pearl of price untold;
Gifts of Paradise all precious,
Stored within the cave, refresh us.

Byzantine Liturgy

May he make us children of God, he who for our sakes wished to become a child of man.   *St. Augustine*

Living the Christmas Season

December 25

All the ends of the earth have seen
the salvation by our God.   Ps 98

At a time of extraordinary peace in the world, the Prince of Peace was born at Bethlehem. It would seem that because of the imperial census the little town was crowded with others who, like Mary and Joseph, had come from their ordinary homes to register in this place of family origin. Hence *there was no place for them in the inn.* Just outside the town, on a hillside, Joseph found shelter in a rock grotto or cave, used as a stable: this tradition comes down to us strongly from St. Justin Martyr, who lived there only a century afterwards. Here at least, even if there was no comfort or luxury, there was privacy. And so, in the silence of that first momentous Christmas night, Mary *gave birth to her firstborn Son and wrapped him in swaddling clothes, and laid him in a manger.* In a few simple words the evangelist describes the tremendous fact that the Son of God was born as man. If we think of the full significance of the role of the second Person of the Blessed Trinity, we cannot but be deeply amazed at the mystery of his condescension in actually becoming a man while remaining God. Let me thank God for this tremendous gift to mankind. O little Babe of Bethlehem, with feelings of deepest reverence and gratitude I adore you as my God and Savior.   *David J. de Burgh, S.D.B.*

―――――――

*O God, who made this most sacred night shine with
the illumination of the true Light, grant that as we
have known the mystery of that Light on earth we
may also perfectly enjoy it in heaven.*

Traditional prayer

―――――――

By the mystery of the Word made flesh the light of
God's glory has shone anew upon the eyes of our mind:
that while we acknowledge him to be God seen by men,
we may be drawn by him to the love of things unseen.

Traditional

December 26

*She gave birth to her first-born Son and wrapped
him in swaddling clothes and laid him in a manger....*

Lk 2

Surely I am filled with awe at the thought that God,
Creator of the world, actually became a tiny human baby,
detaching himself from the rights of his divinity in order
to do so. A baby arouses immediate sympathy and even
delight as we watch it stretching out its little hands to
make contact and share its love. Such was Jesus, too,
stretching out his infant hands to make contact with me,
to invite me into the closest possible intimacy with him
throughout my life—I protecting him, he protecting me!
What confidence in him this thought should inspire! Dear
Jesus, I give You my heart now with all its thoughts and
desires and I ask You to make it entirely Yours for ever.

David J. de Burgh, S.D.B.

Teach, O teach us, holy Child,
By Thy face so meek and mild,
Teach us to resemble Thee,
In Thy sweet humility!
   Hail, Thou ever-blessed morn!
   Hail, redemption's happy dawn!
   Sing through all Jerusalem,
   Christ is born in Bethlehem.

Traditional hymn

Humility is the crib of Jesus. He is born in the humble soul.   *Timothy Giaccardo*

December 27

Joseph went...to register with Mary, his espoused wife, who was with child.   Lk 2

A further thought on Bethlehem concerns obedience. No doubt our Lady would have preferred to remain in her own hometown of Nazareth for the birth of her child. It would have been so much more convenient; she would have been sure of the help of her own mother, relatives and friends. Bethlehem was so very far away for travel in those days. Yet here we see Mary's implicit confidence in God's Providence. We read of no murmur or dissent on her part or that of Joseph. In the decree of the distant Roman Emperor they obeyed also the authority of God, who knew that in this way the scriptural prophecy would be fulfilled regarding the Messiah's birth. How often things occur in my life which I readily dub a "nuisance," "inconvenient," "inconsiderate," and so on, things that upset my comfort or convenience or well-arranged plans.

It is so easy to make a fuss on such occasions. Sometimes objections may be necessary but surely never a fuss, which only shows lack of self-control, a mind too easily disturbed. Is there not much room for improvement in me here? Let me pray to our Lady, asking her to help me to do something practical about it this very day.

David J. de Burgh, S.D.B.

Remember, O most gracious Virgin Mary, that never was it known that anyone who fled to your protection, implored your help, or sought your intercession was left unaided. Inspired by this confidence, I fly to you, O Virgin of virgins, my Mother.

St. Bernard

We look to Mary, knowing that she offers our prayers to Jesus.   *James Alberione*

December 28

Let us go over to Bethlehem and see this event which the Lord has made known to us.   Lk 2

Those wise men of the East were not the first to find Christ, and to offer their gifts. For we know from St. Luke that that wonderful lantern of God shone too on shepherds in the nearby hills of Judea: *And the angel said to them, "Do not be afraid. For behold, I bring you good news of great joy, which shall be to all the people."* And they went in haste, the Scripture tells us, *and they found Mary and Joseph, and the babe lying in the manger.*

What gifts the shepherds brought, St. Luke does not tell us. But in an old play of Catholic England, the shepherds are pictured bringing the Christ Child all they could—a ball to play with, a little bird, and a sprig of holly berries. That is only a legend of course, for the shepherds and the wise men of the East really brought the same gifts—the gifts of themselves—the only gift the Christ Child wants...waits for each of us to bring him.

Richard Cardinal Cushing

Lead me to Thy peaceful manger,
Wond'rous Babe of Bethlehem;
Shepherds hail Thee, yet a stranger;
Let me worship Thee with them.
I am vile, but Thou art holy;
Oh, unite my heart to Thee;
Make me contrite, keep me lowly,
Pure as Thou wouldst have me be.

M. Bridges

See, amid the winter's snow,
Born for us on earth below,
See, the tender Lamb appears,
Promised from eternal years!

E. Coswall

December 29

Simeon...was just and pious, and awaited the consolation of Israel, and the Holy Spirit was upon him.

Lk 2

Holy Simeon is a meaningful figure in the history of the Jews. Just as Zachary and Elizabeth could not have been alone, but must have had many associates, faithful to the true tradition of the Messiah like themselves; just as the families from which Mary and Joseph came could not have been the only faithful households, but must have been associated with many others; so Simeon, and later the prophetess Anna, must have been two among many who were faithful in *looking for the consolation of Israel*. In all times, under all circumstances, underneath the excitements of life which history most loves to record, there has always been, and there still always is, a great ocean of goodness on which the world ultimately relies....

Simeon was *just and devout;* he was true in his life and spiritual in his mind; he was a man of prayer, looking to the great end, and receiving communications from God. He was a contemplative, with a clean heart, and the two qualities gave him all he needed: the power to recognize our Lord when he met him. *Blessed are the clean of heart, for they shall see God.* Such a man is led *by the Spirit;* such a man is tried, but at the end of the trial it is given him to *take the child into his arms, and to bless God.*

+ *Alban Goodier*

━━━━━━━

Grant, we ask you, almighty God, that as we are bathed in the new light of your Incarnate Word, that which shines by faith in our minds may blaze out likewise in our actions.   Traditional prayer

━━━━━━━

From death, from dark, from deafness,
   from despair,
This Life, this Light, this Word, this Joy repairs.

St. Robert Southwell

December 30

Bethlehem-Ephratha...
From you shall come forth for me
    one who is to be ruler in Israel....   Mi 5

Bethlehem means "house of bread"; hence it was a fitting place for the birth of him who was to call himself *the Bread of Life* and to give himself to the world in the form of bread. From the very earliest ages, as far back as can be traced, bread, made from various cereal grains, seems to have been the staple food of mankind. This no doubt was precisely why God chose it for the outward form of the Blessed Eucharist as a common bond of unity for all mankind. Born in the "house of bread," our Savior made his final sacrifice on the cross begin with the breaking of bread at the first eucharistic supper with his apostles. Let me consider now how much I owe to the incarnation of Christ together with the Holy Eucharist. Is my Holy Communion not merely a bond of union with Jesus but also with all his disciples, including those with whom I come in contact? O Sacrament most holy, O Sacrament divine, all praise and all thanksgiving be every moment thine!   *David J. de Burgh, S.D.B.*

———————

Give us our daily bread,
    O God, the Bread of strength—
For we have learned to know
    How weak we are at length.
                    Adelaide A. Procter

———————

Only love explains the Eucharistic Mystery.
                      James Alberione

The Lord called me from birth,
and from my mother's womb he gave me my name.

Is 49

We must go over to Bethlehem. We must seek Christ. We must accept him. We must proclaim in our lives that as he loved all men, so we must love all men for love of him. We must show a cynical world that the charity in our hearts and the security in our lives and the glowing eagerness in our faces are based upon our knowledge and love and service of a God whose ways are not ours.

We must rejoice in the very fact that by accepting God on God's terms we gain the greatest gift of all, the receiving of God's love and our elevation to the supernatural and extraordinary dignity of sons of God, heirs of heaven and brothers of Christ.

In all humility we seek out the Babe of Bethlehem, kneel at his feet in homage, promise him that we shall accept him on his terms. Then with heads erect to look up to the God who loves us, with eyes aglow as we see God in everyone, with hearts on fire with love for God and others, with eager steps to carry out God's mission, with a song in our souls, we wish one and all a blessed Christmas Season. Christ came to bring blessings to the world. In his plan we are to help him.

Richard Cardinal Cushing

―――――――――――――

Jesus, the Ransomer of man,
Who, ere created light began,
Didst from the sovereign Father spring,
His power and glory equaling.
The Father's light and splendor Thou,

Their endless hope to Thee that bow;
Accept the prayers and praise today
That through the world Thy servants pay.

Traditional hymn

———————

O wondrous humility, in which all the greatness of God lay hid!   *St. Augustine*

January 1

When the designated time had come, God sent forth his Son born of a woman....   Gal 4

Today the Church of Mary's Son celebrates the feast of Mary, the Mother of God. The Church also celebrates today as the Day of Peace. These two celebrations go well together because peace enters the heart of man when man does what Mary did even as Mother of God: she did what God asked her to do.

At the annunciation she was told by the angel that God had chosen her to be the Mother of his Son. All God asked of Mary was her free consent to his choice. Her final answer to God was: *Behold the handmaid of the Lord. Be it done unto me according to your word.*

Because of her faith, Mary's heart was set on doing the will of God. In the light of the same faith, she could see that in God's will is the happiness, the joy, and the peace of heart for which all of us yearn.

Mary was free to obey, she was free to love, she was free to live and to be at peace. She was at peace with God. It is the Mother of God who invites us today to follow her way of faith and simplicity and trust to joy and to peace.

Humberto Cardinal Medeiros

Hail, Mother of mercy,
Mother of God and Mother of pardon,
Mother of hope and Mother of grace,
Mother full of holy joy—
O Mary!   Salve Mater

Mary's joy is to console her children.

James Alberione

Epiphany

"We observed his star at its rising and have come to
pay him homage."   Mt 2

The magi had brought with them symbolic gifts fit for
a king, three of the gifts then considered most valuable in
the East. Imagine their surprise, then, when the star
stopped *over the place where the child was.* But Scripture
simply states: *...going into the house, they saw the child with*
Mary his mother, and they fell down and worshiped him. Then,
opening their treasures, they offered him gifts, gold and frankin-
cense and myrrh. How often when we say we are eager to
do God's will, we show not only surprise but even resent-
ment when eventually it is manifested in a way contrary
to our likings. Do we then refuse him our gifts of resigna-
tion, submission and acceptance?

When was the last time I put up a struggle against the
manifest will of God? Was it worth it? Did I gain peace of
mind by kicking against the goad? Perhaps in the future it
may help me to bring Mary into the picture. The magi, we
read, *saw the child with Mary his mother.* If I find any duty
or task difficult or something hard to accept, let me ask
Mary's help to bow down humbly to the wise will of God,

and then carry it out cheerfully. Let me reflect now on what attitudes of my mind should correspond with the magi's gifts of gold, frankincense and myrrh. What practical form can I give these points for the day ahead?

David J. de Burgh, S.D.B.

―――――――

Mary, dear Mother, help me in this useful search, so that I may "return to my own country" of God's will by a way that is completely other than any previous obstinacy and self-will....

David J. de Burgh, S.D.B.

―――――――

After the humble shepherds, there came to the manger the great and the powerful—great men who yet knew how to humble themselves.   *James Alberione*

Baptism of the Lord

Here is my servant whom I uphold,
  my chosen one with whom I am pleased....

Is 42

The baptism of Jesus marked the start of his public life, and the words of the Father signify both his twofold role of suffering and serving and the divine delight in his presence on earth. This was for Jesus an identification with mankind and with the Father's redemptive will. In the dove, moreover, we see the symbol of the third Person of the Trinity, the Holy Spirit. Here, then, we have an almost tangible evidence of the most Holy Trinity.

At my baptism the same elements were present, not merely the water but the three divine Persons effecting the essential sacrament. On that day too, the Father proclaimed: *This is my beloved son with whom I am well pleased.* But have I remained faithful to the grace and opportunities then received? Have I never taken away God's pleasure from my soul? Have I tried to exclude suffering and serving in the cause of God and my fellowmen? Baptism was meant to make me "another Christ." How am I measuring up to that ideal?   *David J. de Burgh, S.D.B.*

O Jesus, baptized for me, cleanse my soul from the last traces of accumulated sin. Help me to start again, generously, to be faithful to my baptismal vocation. Let me start today to be constantly pleasing to you.   David J. de Burgh, S.D.B.

We will be happy and serene if we always do what the Lord wants, day by day, moment by moment.
Mother Thecla Merlo

Christmas Novena

December 16–24

Brief History

This novena in preparation for Christmas, composed by Rev. Charles Vachetta, C.M., in 1721, was first sung in the Church of the Immaculate in Turin, northern Italy. Father Vachetta took most of the material for it from the Old Testament prophecies, which refer to the coming of the Redeemer, and from the Psalms. Particularly interesting is the canticle, "Let the Heavens Be Glad" which he composed from various phrases of Sacred Scripture.

In a short time the novena became popular throughout Italy as well as in many other parts of the world.

It begins on December 16, nine days before the Feast of the Nativity, and ends on Christmas Eve.

Christmas Novena

Leader

Our Lord and King is drawing near, O come, let us adore him.

All *Our Lord and King is drawing near, O come, let us adore him.*

Leader

Rejoice, O daughter of Zion and exult fully, O daughter of Jerusalem! Behold, the Lord and Master comes, and there shall be a brilliant light in that day, and the mountains shall drop down sweetness, and hills flow with milk and honey, for in that day the Great Prophet will come, and he will renew Jerusalem.

All *Our Lord and King, etc.*

Leader

Behold, the God-man of the house of David will come to sit upon the royal throne, and you will see him and your heart will rejoice.

All *Our Lord and King, etc.*

Leader

Behold, the Lord our Protector will come to save us, Israel's holy One, wearing the crown of royalty. He will exercise his rule from sea to shining sea, and from the waters of the river to the ends of the earth.

All *Our Lord and King, etc.*

Leader

Behold, the Lord and King will appear, and He will not deceive; but if he should delay, wait for him; he will surely come and will not tarry.

All *Our Lord and King, etc.*

Leader

The Lord will come down like rain upon the fleece of Gideon; justice will thrive and an abundance of true peace; all the kings of the earth will adore him, and every nation will serve him.

All *Our Lord and King, etc.*

Leader

A child will be born to us, and he will be called God the Almighty; he will sit upon the throne of David his father, and he will hold sway, the sign of his power on his shoulder.

All *Our Lord and King, etc.*

Leader

Bethlehem, city of the Most High God, from you will come forth the King of Israel. He will proceed forth from his eternity; he will be praised in the midst of the entire universe; there will be peace in our land when he comes.

All *Our Lord and King, etc.*

(On the Eve of Christmas add:)

Leader

Tomorrow the wickedness of the world will be destroyed, and over us will reign the Savior of the world.

All *Our Lord and King, etc.*

Leader

Near at last is Christ our King.

All *O come, let us adore him.*

Let the Heavens Be Glad

Let the heavens be glad and the earth rejoice.
    O all you mountains, praise the Lord.
Drop down dew from above, you heavens,
    and let the clouds rain the Just One.
Let the earth be opened,
    and bud forth the Savior.

Remember us, O Lord,
 and visit us in your salvation.
Show your mercy to us, O Lord,
 and grant us your salvation.
Send forth, O Lord, the Lamb, the Ruler of the earth,
 from the rock in the desert to the mount of Zion.
Come to free us, O Lord, God of hosts;
 show your face, and we shall be saved.
Come, O Lord, and visit us in peace,
 so that we may rejoice before you with a perfect heart.
May we know on earth, O Lord, your Way,
 your salvation among all nations.
Put forth, O Lord, your strength,
 and come to save us.
Come, O Lord, and do not hesitate;
 pardon the sins of your people.
O that you would rend the heavens and come down,
 the mountains would melt in your presence.
Come, and show us your face, O Lord,
 you who sit upon the cherubim.
Glory be to the Father, etc.

Hymn

Lo! now a thrilling voice sounds forth,
And chides the darkened shades of earth.
Away pale dreams, dim shadows fly,
Christ in his might does shine on high.

The Lamb of God is sent below,
Himself to pay the debt we owe,
Oh! for this gift let every voice
With heartfelt songs and tears rejoice.

The Blessed Author of all time
Took mortal form to free from crime.
Lest lost should be those whom he made,
And with his flesh, our ransom paid.

And lo! with heavenly grace instilled,
A mother's bosom chaste is filled.
Behold a Virgin's body bears,
The mystery of endless years.

His home he makes her spotless breast.
O temple meet, for God to rest.
Inviolate, this holy one
Conceives and bears the eternal Son!

To him who comes the world to free,
To God, the Son, all glory be:
To God, the Father, as is meet,
To God, the Blessed Paraclete. Amen.

Biblical Readings

December 16: Genesis 3:1-15; Romans 1:18-26

December 17: Genesis 3:14-20; Romans 5:12-21

December 18: Genesis 17:15-23; Romans 4:13-23

December 19: Deuteronomy 15:13-20; Acts 3:18-26

December 20: Isaiah 28:14-20; Romans 10:5-11

December 21: 1 Samuel 2:1-10; Luke 1:26-39

December 22: Deuteronomy 7:6-21; Ephesians 2:12-22

December 23: Isaiah 7:10-16; Matthew 1:18-25

December 24: Micah 5:1-5; Luke 2:1-8

Leader

Drop down dew from above, O you heavens, and let the clouds rain the just One.

All *Let the earth be opened, and bud forth the Savior.*

Daily Antiphons for the Magnificat.

December 16: Behold, the King will come, the Lord of the earth, and he will free us from the yoke of our captivity.

December 17: O Wisdom, proceeding from the mouth of the Most High, you reach from end to end and order all things mightily and sweetly. Come to guide us in the way of prudence.

December 18: O Lord and Leader of the house of Israel, you spoke to Moses from a flaming bush and on Sinai gave him the law. Come to redeem us with your out-stretched arm.

December 19: O root of Jesse, raised as a standard for the people, before whom kings and nations will bow in silence: come to deliver us without delay.

December 20: O Key of David, scepter of Israel, you open and no one closes, close and no one opens. Come to free mankind from its bonds in prison, where it sits in darkness and the shadow of death.

December 21: O Radiant Dawn, splendor of eternal light and Sun of justice: come to enlighten those who sit in darkness and the shadow of death.

December 22: O King of nations and their desired one, the cornerstone that unites them all: come to rescue poor mankind, whom you formed from dust.

December 23: O Emmanuel, our King and Lawgiver, the Expected of the nations and their Savior: come to deliver us, O Lord our God.

December 24: With the rising of the sun, you will see the King of kings and Lord of lords coming from his Father, like a bridegroom from his bridal chamber.

Magnificat

Antiphon:

My soul proclaims the greatness of the Lord
And joy fills my spirit in God my Savior.

He has looked with love on His lowly handmaid
And every generation will call me blessed.

God almighty has done great things for me.
Holy is his name.

His mercy extends through every age
On all those who fear him.

He has shown the might of his arm
And scattered the proud of heart.

He has thrust the mighty off their thrones
And has raised on high the lowly.

To the hungry he has given food,
But the rich go away so empty.

He has helped his servant, Israel
And has never forgotten his mercy.

He promised mercy to our fathers,
To Abraham and his offspring forever.

Glory....

(Repeat the antiphon.)

Prayer

Leader

Hasten, we beseech you, O Lord; do not delay. Grant
us the help of supernatural virtue, so that your coming
will be a consolation to those who hope in your mercy.
You who live and reign with God the Father in the unity
of the Holy Spirit, God world without end.

All Amen.

Celebrating the Advent-Christmas Seasons

✿✿✿✿✿✿✿✿
ADVENT
SHARING

It seems that the message and the meaning of Advent are more pronounced today in our churches. And, as it should be, we are asked to participate in the preparation for Christmas and to leave the office, home and institutional parties until *after* we have heralded the birth of Christ.

This affords us the opportunity to teach and work with our children. Our hearts and minds may center on the joy of instilling in these young, beautiful minds, the true meaning of Christmas, without the obligation of centering our attention on adult parties.

It is an ideal time to introduce our youngsters, whether as a class, a portion of a class or our own children and neighborhood children to better understand the part God wishes them to play in the happiness of others.

The first Sunday of Advent is an ideal time to take children to a nursing home. Let them adopt one adult whom they will assist during the Christmas season. Although many of these patients can no longer address their greeting cards, this does not mean that the need to contact dear friends and relatives has passed. Teach the children to fulfill this task for the elderly.

On the following pages we will suggest a number of items, many of which are simple to make and easy to distribute to residents of nursing homes or to shut-ins. There are so many lonely, helpless people who rely solely on the visiting nurse's call. You may obtain some names of such people from the pastor or a nurses' agency so that you can introduce your child or class group to the real joy of Christmas.

Arthritic hands need help to trim a small tree. Help is required in wrapping gifts.... If you ask around, you'll find many places where you can make a difference.

THE JESSE TREE

This traditional advent decoration is another reminder of the long years of waiting for the Savior.

Children will delight in helping Mom and Dad at home or their teacher at school with tracing and cutting out the symbols of the Jesse tree. These should be hung on a small tree for full impact.

The Jesse tree dates back at least to twelfth-century France, where it made its appearance in a stain-glass window of the famed Abbey of St. Denis. The tree derives its name from Jesse, the father of King David. The medieval Jesse tree—very popular in the great cathedrals of the thirteenth century—was wrought in stained-glass and presented portraits of Jesus' royal ancestors, with Jesse reposing at the base and Christ enthroned on the top. Christ was surrounded by doves representing the Seven Gifts of the Holy Spirit described in one of the Immanuel prophecies of Isaiah (11:2, 3). The contemporary tree is usually three-dimensional and bears symbols of salvation history from the fall of our first parents to the coming of Christ.

To make a Jesse tree, "plant" an ordinary branch in a sand-filled flower pot and hang from it symbols of Christ, his ancestors and other important Old Testament personalities. (The symbol of Christ is placed at the top, with that of Mary just beneath. The symbol of Adam and Eve goes near the base of the tree, with the other symbols moving up the tree in chronological order.)

Making a Jesse tree is a good way of learning or reviewing salvation history. The following illustrations and explanations may prove helpful in sharing this meaningful custom with the children:

Adam and Eve

The fruit stands for our first parents' sin of disobedience. (If your children ask questions, explain that the sin was serious because God gave a serious and definite command which Adam and Eve knowingly and willfully disobeyed; this is the meaning of the forbidden fruit narrative in the Bible.)

Noah

The children will probably have heard of Noah and the ark. The rainbow was sent by God as a sign of his friendship with man.

Abraham and Sarah

Abraham and his wife Sarah were very old and did not have any children. They did not have a

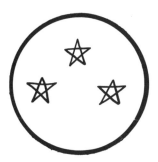

regular home, either. They lived in a tent. God told them that the people who would descend from them would be so many that they could not be counted. "They will be like the stars in the sky or the grains of sand on the seashore," God said. He also promised Abraham and Sarah that their descendants would have houses and cities in the land God had chosen for them. Abraham believed God, and because of this, God rewarded him with special blessings.

Isaac

Isaac was the son of Abraham and Sarah. He was born when they were very old. One day God asked Abraham to take Isaac's life by offering him in sacrifice on an altar. Abraham felt very sad, but he got ready to obey God. Then God told Abraham *not* to offer his son. God had only been testing Abraham's obedience. He was very pleased that Abraham was willing to obey him.

Jacob

Jacob was the son of Isaac. His other name was Israel. One day a prophet looked into the future. He said, "A star will rise out of Jacob." He meant that the Savior of the world would be one of Jacob's descendants.

Judah

Jacob had twelve sons. When he was dying, he blessed them all, one by one. He called Judah a lion, because Judah was very brave. The Savior was going to come from Judah's family.

Ruth

Ruth was a very good young woman. She did not belong to God's people, but she met a good man of the family of Judah while she was harvesting grain. She married this man. Their grandson was Jesse, after whom our tree is nàmed.

Jesse

Jesse lived in the town of Bethlehem. He owned a large flock of sheep. Jesse had several sons. The youngest son became the most famous (David).

David

David was the best and greatest king of God's people except for Jesus himself. What symbols could we use for King David? (These symbols could include a crown for a king, a harp to stand for the psalms or prayer-songs David wrote, a slingshot for his triumph over Goliath, and the Hebrew star named after him.)

Solomon

Solomon was one of David's sons. He built a beautiful temple to God, as his father had asked him to do. He decorated this temple with shining candlesticks, vases and bowls—all of pure gold. Solomon knew that God deserves the very best we can give him.

Hezekiah

Hezekiah was also a king. He was a descendant of David and Solomon, and he tried to love God the way David did. One day the prophet Isaiah came to Hezekiah and told him he would soon die. Hezekiah felt sad, because people at that time did not know about heaven. As soon as Isaiah had left, Hezekiah began to cry and pray to the Lord to let him live longer. In a few minutes the prophet came back and told Hezekiah, "The Lord says, 'I have heard your prayer and seen your tears. You will live fifteen years longer'" (possible symbol—teardrops).

Josiah

Josiah was another good king. He wanted to serve God well. One day an important scroll was found that told about God's law. Josiah called his people together and they all promised to keep the law of God.

Mary

Now we come to Mary, the Mother of Jesus, and for her we need an especially wonderful symbol. One of the symbols we could use is a beautiful lily. Another is a wild rose, which has five petals.

Jesus

For Jesus, of course, we should have a very special crown, because he is the greatest King of all. We might put a Chi-Rho (say Key-Row or Kye-Row) on the crown. The Chi-Rho is a Greek abbreviation for the name Christ. Can you think of some other symbols we could use for Jesus?

Other familiar Old Testament figures who could be represented on the Jesse tree are: Joseph, brother of Judah (many-colored coat); Moses (burning bush and tablets of the commandments); the major prophets—Isaiah, Jeremiah, Ezekiel and Daniel (scrolls)

Joseph

Moses

Prophets

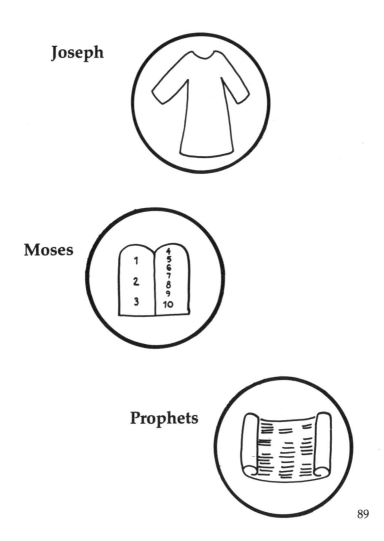

The Advent Calendar

This custom began in Germany and has now spread widely into other countries. While there are many varieties of commercial Advent calendars, these calendars usually consist of a colorful scene printed on a large piece of cardboard that is set up at the beginning of Advent. Every day the children open one window of the scene to reveal a picture or symbol of the coming feast of Christmas. Then, at last, on December 24, the main door is opened, showing the nativity scene.

Advent calendars are a means of reminding the children of the spiritual task of preparing their souls for the feast of Christmas.

Because we are dealing with children, we must also consider the commercial aspect, remembering that little hearts beat in anticipation of Santa and surprise gifts. More than once a day you will be asked, "How many more days until Christmas?"

A simple calendar may be made at home or at school. On a sheet of stiff paper, rule out enough calendar squares for the month of December (or include the days of November that are part of the Advent Season). Number the squares. As each day goes by, the children can put a Christmas seal or sticker in the appropriate square. It would be fitting

December 19—						
			1	2	3	4
5	6	7	8	9	10	11
12	13	14	15	16	17	18
19	20	21	22	23	24	25
26	27	28	29	30	31	

to read or discuss Christmas themes each day before attaching the sticker. In this way, the children are prepared for both the spiritual and family celebration of Christmas, but will be assured of an emphasis on the Birth of Christ.

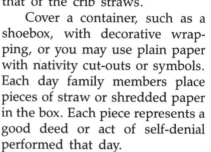

CRIB STRAWS

In conjunction with the Advent calendar, another practice which youngsters will cherish is that of the crib straws.

Cover a container, such as a shoebox, with decorative wrapping, or you may use plain paper with nativity cut-outs or symbols. Each day family members place pieces of straw or shredded paper in the box. Each piece represents a good deed or act of self-denial performed that day.

On Christmas Eve, that "straw" is placed in the manger and becomes the bed for Baby Jesus. Our behavior thus determines how soft or hard the bed will be, how well prepared we are to welcome him.

THE ADVENT WREATH

Originally, Advent wreaths may have been cart wheels, wound with greens and decorated with lights, strung up in the halls of the sun-worshiping tribes of northern Europe.

The Christians preparing for their feast of light and life, the nativity of the Savior, found this wheel or wreath an appropriate means. Adding one light for each of the four Sundays in Advent, they would think about the darkness without God after the fall, and the growing hope for salvation. This hope was enkindled in Eden and nourished through the ages by the prophets up to John, the precursor, who announced the coming of the Son.

The wreath without beginning or end stands for eternity; the evergreens, for everlasting life; the four candles represent the ages "sitting in the darkness and shadow of death." Each candle adds more light until on Christmas the light from the wreath sets off, as it were, a blaze of light on the "tree of life," the Christmas tree, for the time is fulfilled.

A ready-made Christmas wreath may be used, or evergreen may be twined about a circle of wire. The wreath is placed on a table top or suspended from a light fixture by purple ribbons.

The wreath contains four candles, evenly spaced—three purple and one pink. (If you only have white candles or are making your own, purple and pink designs may be drawn on them with melted wax crayons, or a non-combustible pink or purple ribbon may be tied around each.) Purple stands for penance and pink for joy. During the first week, only one purple candle is lighted at the beginning of the evening meal or at prayer time; the next week, two; the third week, the pink also; and the fourth week, all four.

The purpose of the wreath is to remind us of the many centuries that passed while the world was waiting for the Savior. Each candle represents a period of time.

The Advent Wreath Ceremony

The ceremony is simple. It starts at the evening meal on the Saturday before the first Sunday in Advent with the blessing of the wreath.

(The head of the household is the one designated to say the prayers, following which various members of the family light the candles. If the group is not a family, then a leader may be selected to say the prayers and others appointed to light the candles.)

Blessing the Wreath

Parent or Leader:

O God, by whose word all things are sanctified, pour forth your blessing upon this wreath, and grant that we who use it may prepare our hearts for the coming of Christ and may receive from you abundant graces. Through Christ our Lord. Amen.

The First Week

Parent or Leader:

O Lord, stir up your might, we beg you, and come, that by your protection we may deserve to be rescued from the threatening dangers of our sins and be saved by your deliverance. Through Christ our Lord. Amen.

Each night the first purple candle is lit by the youngest child of the household and is left burning during the meal.

Then the evening meal prayer follows.

The Second Week

Parent or Leader:

O Lord, stir up our hearts that we may prepare for your only begotten Son, that through his coming we may be made worthy to serve you with pure minds. Through Christ our Lord. Amen.

Then the eldest child lights not only the first, but a second purple candle. Both candles burn during the evening meal as before.

The Third Week

The joyful Sunday in Advent, known as "Gaudete," is represented by rose (or pink) instead of the penitential purple color. Each night during the third week the mother of the family lights the pink, as well as the two previously burned purple candles, after the following prayer has been said.

Parent or Leader:

O Lord, we beg you, incline your ear to our prayers and enlighten the darkness of our minds by the grace of your visitation. Through Christ our Lord. Amen.

Following the meal the three candles are extinguished.

The Fourth Week

After repeating the following prayer, the head of the household lights all four candles in proper sequence during the fourth week.

Parent or Leader:

O Lord, stir up your power, we pray, and come; with great might help us, that with the help of your grace, your merciful forgiveness may hasten what our sins impede. Through Christ our Lord. Amen.

Candles can be replaced as necessary during a particular Advent Season without re-blessing the wreath.

HYMN

O Come, O come, Emmanuel,
And ransom captive Israel,
That mourns in lonely exile here,
Until the Son of God appear.
Rejoice, Rejoice, O Israel,
To thee shall come Emmanuel.

After Advent

For the Christmas Season, which follows immediately after Advent, candles and ribbons can be changed to white. If you wish, the wreath itself can be freshened with new greens and decorated festively for use during the holiday period. Lighting all four white candles to burn during the principal meal each day of the Christmas Season is a customary and appropriate practice.

CHRISTMAS ANGEL

On the following pages, you will find decorations easily made by children to enhance the meaning of Christmas.

The days before Christmas may be tense ones for children. Their anticipation of the holiday makes them restless. This is an opportune time to teach the reason for this season. It is a time for children to absorb the spirit of Christmas and to make lasting memories for themselves and for you.

Angels and Christmas go together, so let us start our project with the simplest paper angel. You may use the pattern given here or vary it according to personal taste.

You will need colored construction paper or silver or gold foil.

Cut out the body and a pair of wings. You may use one color for wings and body or make the wings a different color.

With glue or a stapler, attach the wings, with one slightly forward of the other. Now you will need a thread to run through the body at the point where the angel will balance.

There it is, ready to hang. A group of these will make a choir of angels.

DECORATIVE BELLS

Perhaps a walk with Dad, Mom, or another family member will provide the evergreen boughs. At home, spray two yogurt cups, or two orange juice cans with gold paint or whatever color you choose. Punch a hole in the bottom of each. Tie a large red bow around the boughs to hold them together. Insert the end of each ribbon into the cup or can. Tie a large knot so the ribbon will not slip through. This makes a lovely welcome for your own home or that of a neighbor.

Centuries before Christ, people who worshiped nature brought evergreens into their homes during festival time as proof of continuing life.

CHRISTMAS CANDLES

Someone once said that Christmas is candle glow, and I personally believe I'd find Christmas joy being a bit incomplete without the presence of glowing candles.

Before beginning the directions, perhaps a reminder is in order that heated wax can be dangerous. Children should not be near the place where wax is being melted. Instead, they can share in the finishing touches of this candle.

You will need:

- 2 boxes of paraffin wax.
- a piece of string 1½ inches longer than the paraffin box (for the wick).
- Your choice of trimmings: sequins, candle glitter, a piece of plastic holly with berries, or a picture cut from an old Christmas card.

Melt one box of the paraffin wax in the top of a double boiler over very hot water.

There are usually four bars of wax in each box. Separate the bars. Ladle melted wax between bars 1 and 2, and press them together. Place the string which you have soaked in the melted wax over bar 2 so that you have ¾ inch protruding from what you want to be the top of your candle. (See illustration on page 101.) Now repeat the process by ladling hot wax on bar 2, placing bar 3

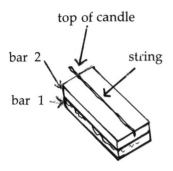

top of candle

bar 2

string

bar 1

over it and with more warm wax between them, press bar 4 next to bar 3. Any excess that oozes from the sides is all right.

The next step is to beat the remaining warm wax in the double boiler until the wax looks like whipped cream. Working quickly, adhere this whipped wax to all four sides of the candle. When it has cooled, use straight or dressmaker pins to decorate as you wish. A sprig of plastic holly is most effective, as is candle glitter. The glow from this candle as the center burns down is very homey and "Christmasy."

BOOTIE FOR BABY JESUS

diagram 1   diagram 2

Another popular and simple decoration is that of the Christmas bootie. Perhaps before beginning the project, a few words about Mary's preparation for the coming of her Son would add more meaning and also stir up young imaginations. The children will also be drawn into a deeper realization that Jesus was born into a family, the holiest family ever.

To make the bootie, you will need:

- an empty liquid soap bottle (preferably white or transparent)
- cotton balls (8 for each bootie)
- glue
- approximately 14 inches of red or green ribbon for each bootie
- scissors
- paper punch

First, cut off the top of the soap bottle about 3¼ inches from the bottom (diagram 1). The top half of the bottle may be discarded.

With scissors, make two slightly angular cuts to form a flap as shown. Punch holes on each side near flap (diagram 2).

Tuck the flap in, thread ribbon through the holes and then tie. Glue cotton along the top of the bootie.

You may wish to fill the bootie with Christmas candy and give it to someone special!

THE THREE WISE MEN

Here is the opportunity for children to use the brightest colors in their imagination.

You will need only construction paper and glue to complete this project. When we think of kings, we think of reds, blues, purple and gold, but perhaps you have other colors to mix and match for these Wise Men who were searching for Christ.

From a 9" square of construction paper cut a quarter of a circle shape as show in the illustration and roll it into a cone. This will be the body of the king.

Now cut a cape from a different color according to the pattern shown. Fasten it around the shoulders of the king. Just a spot of glue will fasten the cape as you overlap the points to form a smooth, curved line from the back to the front.

Using the same color, cut the crown from the pattern. Just overlap the two points, fasten with glue and slip over the point of the cone. A dab of glue will secure it there.

And soon enough we have Three Wise Men making their way to Bethlehem across our fireplace mantle or windowsill.

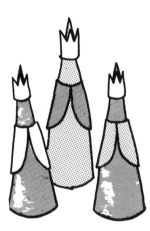

(Pattern on next page.)

ACTUAL SIZE

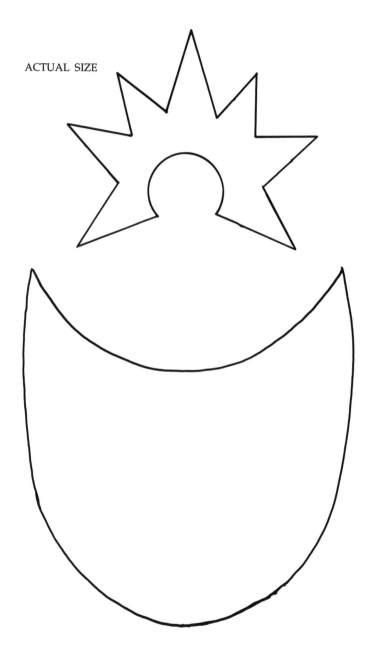

CHRISTMAS POSTERS

Many of us save Christmas cards. After all, they are too pretty to discard. Yet, before we know it, it's time for a new round of them. Good news! You have done well to save those cards because now is the time to make excellent use of them.

With some construction paper, a pair of scissors, and a bit of glue, your children will find that Christmas cards will keep them busy making Christmas posters for an entire stormy day.

The children may make their posters on one theme, such as carolers, candles, trees, etc., or they can tell the Christmas story with a nativity scene surrounded by any of the above. It will take a while to find the right cut-outs needed for the picture one decides to make, but an interchange of cards from a group will make this activity a joy. Perhaps each child could be asked to tell a story of the poster he or she has created.

CHRISTMAS PLACE CARDS

Again, we rely on cut-outs from Christmas cards. We need plain white cards 4" square. (Construction paper will also do.) Fold the paper in half. Taking a cut-out, glue it off-center, leaving room for a name. What a lovely addition to your table is this simple card made with the love of a child. Christmas, after all, is love.

A CHRISTMAS TABLEAU

Your Christmas tableau can be as simple or as extravagant as you wish.

You will need cardboard or a backdrop made from old sheets, drapes or whatever material you wish to use.

A child is dressed as Joseph, another as Mary, and a doll should be placed in a manger.

Shepherds, too, can be added, and if this is being done after Christmas then you may also choose to have three Wise Men.

The children stand still while the audience—be it family, school peers, or visitors—sing appropriate religious Christmas carols.

If the characters wiggle a bit, that's quite acceptable. The naturalness of the youngsters adds to the warmth of this Christmas Season.

THE MANGER SCENE

The representation of the Child in the manger goes back to the early centuries of Christianity. For example, a nativity scene from about the year of 380 may be seen in the Catacombs of St. Sebastian in Rome.

The three-dimensional manger scene as we know it today is believed to have originated with St. Francis of Assisi in the thirteenth century. Francis had visited the Holy Land and had seen the Savior's birthplace with his own eyes. Sometime after his return to Italy, he was taken by a great desire to celebrate Christmas in the poverty of a simple stable. So in the forest near the Italian town of Greccio a manger was prepared and filled with hay; a live ox and donkey were brought; and Midnight Mass was celebrated there in the open, by the light of candles and torches.

The family crib scene might be set up a few days before Christmas (without the infant and the Magi), with the recitation of the following prayer:

We ask you, heavenly Father,
to bless this crib which honors
*   your only Son,*
the Word made flesh.
As we think about the birth of
*   your Son*
during this holy season,

lead us to grow in faith
and fill us with your glory.
This we ask through your Son,
our Lord Jesus Christ.
Amen!

On Christmas Eve the Infant is placed in the manger and the shepherds gather about. Soon after Christmas the three kings begin to move toward the stable, which they will reach on the feast of Epiphany.

THE CHRISTMAS TREE

It is common knowledge that Germany is credited with the Christmas tree as we know it today. However, it was not until the nineteenth century that its picturesqueness and charm spread throughout Europe. In the eyes of a child, the tree is without doubt the most delightful of all the season's customs.

A simple program can make the decorating of the family tree an annual celebration and add more meaning to this delightful event.

You could start by asking a child to compose a short prayer for the blessing of the tree. If this is done in a classroom the child may read his own prayer; at home its meaning might be more significant if read by one of the parents.

Each family member or classroom student could then attach a handmade decoration to the tree. This decoration or ornament may be the product of a previous assignment and should be of a religious nature. Together, with hands joined, the singing of carols (including "O Christmas Tree") would be appropriate.

Now let each finish the decorating with other traditional ornaments. Follow this with snacks after the lighting of the tree. You'll find this celebration a memorable experience, and surely the children will not forget it either.

GIFT GIVING

Did you know that you can package the warm glow from your family room or kitchen, wrap it with cellophane and ribbons and share it with someone who may need cheering over the holidays?

It need not be elaborate and should never cost so much as to embarrass the recipient. Many of the activities in this section are simply gift ideas.

Our faith demands that we love our neighbor. With this in mind, we know our gifts should be from the heart. They should be tokens of sharing and consideration, never a thoughtless obligation, and above all they must transmit our sentiments of love.

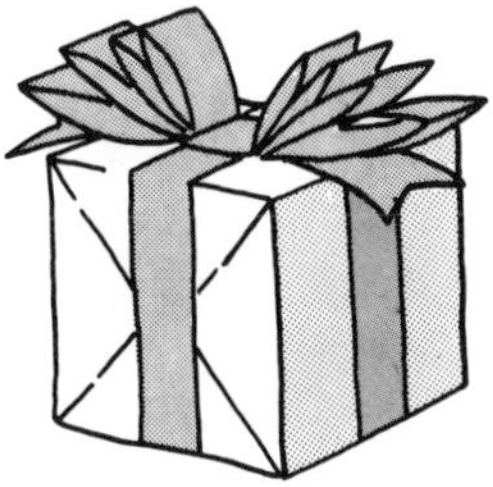

Another thoughtful idea is to mail a package to someone who doesn't expect one. Imagine *your* joy in knowing that you have created a rainbow in some surprised soul. That's the meaning of Christmas—sharing—and who can measure which one has received the warmest glow—the giver or the receiver?

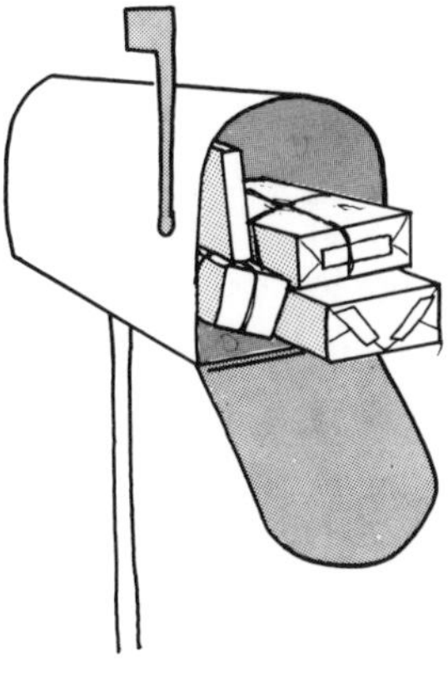

"For somehow, not only at Christmas,
but all the long year through,
The joy that you give to others
is the joy that comes back to you."

John Greenleaf Whittier

POMANDER BALLS

The pomander dates back to Queen Elizabeth I, who carried a scepter in one hand and a pomander in the other. Nowadays, we don't carry them about but hang them in our closets where they impart a delightful scent and drive away moths. Properly made, they last from two to ten years.

These should be made a month in advance, so perhaps they could be the first Advent project.

You will need:
• 1 orange, lemon or lime
• whole cloves
• ground cinnamon

Insert the cloves in the skin of the fruit until the entire surface of the fruit is covered. Do not put the cloves in a straight line as this is apt to crack the skin. Place a heaping teaspoon of ground cinnamon in a small bag with the studded fruit. Shake the bag to coat well. Wrap the fruit loosely or place in a foil-covered box or basket. Store in a dry place until the fruit shrinks and hardens, usually three to four weeks. Remove and wrap with a piece of net and tie with a colored ribbon for hanging or placing in a bureau drawer. The very pleasant aroma will be a reminder of your kindness for a long, long time.

✹✹✹✹✹✹✹✹✹✹
STUFFED
DATES

Here we have a very simple gift but one that the family may work together on or a child might do alone with a minimum of supervision.

You will need a box of pitted dates or you may remove the pits yourself.

Place a walnut half in the center of each date, roll in granulated sugar. Place on waxed paper in a greeting card box or any low-edged container. A piece of plastic holly or a small Christmas decoration of your choosing may be nestled among the dates. Cover with cellophane wrap and tie with a ribbon or bow. This makes a thoughtful gift for sharing a bit of Christmas love.

When you teach your children about sharing, gift giving and family value—these lessons are gifts too.

❈❈❈❈❈❈❈❈❈❈❈

Holiday
Cupcakes

The main object of this activity is to share the experience as a group or as a family. Sometimes we may feel that these types of projects are too much bother and perhaps too difficult for our children. But all of us bake simple cupcakes at one time or another. Just make your regular cupcakes, and have a variety of decorations available. Let your children decorate the iced cupcakes with sprinkles, candies, a trim of colored icing. It's not a matter of expecting perfection, of course. Give guidance where needed and then stand back to admire the finished product.

PUFFED-RICE GOODIES

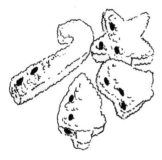

This recipe will call for a little help from you, and with an imagination, you may add other ingredients that you like best: candied fruit, colorful M&M's, nuts, chocolate chips or a combination of the above.

Ingredients:
- ¼ cup margarine
- 10 oz. bag of marshmallows
- 5 cups of popcorn, crispy rice or puffed rice cereal

Melt margarine over low heat in a large saucepan. Add marshmallows, stirring the mixture until marshmallows are melted and well blended. Remove from heat and stir in popcorn or cereal and any other desired ingredients until well coated.

Mold into desired shapes or press lightly into well-buttered baking pans. Decorate with sprinkles or other candied decorations while warm, or wait until cooled; cut into squares if a pan was used; and decorate with frosting. Wrap in plastic wrap and store in a cool place.

EASY CHRISTMAS COOKIES

In all the hustle and bustle of Christmas preparations, some quick and easy recipes are welcome relief. The following can easily be a project involving youngsters too.

Ingredients:
- 1 cup shortening
- 1 cup sugar
- 3½ cups flour
- 2 eggs
- 2 tsps. vanilla
- 2 tsps. baking powder

Oven: 375°
Time: 8 to 12 minutes

Cream shortening and sugar. Add eggs and vanilla. Sift flour and baking powder and add to the creamed mixture. Roll ¼" thick and cut out with Christmas cookie cutters. Before baking in a 375° oven for 8-12 minutes, brush with egg white and sprinkle with colored sugars, or leave plain and after the cookies have cooled decorate with icing, using your own imagination. Makes 3 dozen.

Make your gift package suitable for the person receiving the gift. Cut down oatmeal boxes, etc., to the size desired. Cover with contact paper, or glue appropriate Christmas wrapping on the box and cover. Line with foil or waxed paper, then carefully place the cookies inside. Now all you need is a pretty bow on the top.

If your gift is going to a plantlover, use an attractive planter, cover with cellophane wrap and tie on your bow and gift card.

A canning jar makes a very attractive and practical gift holder.

Save empty coffee cans the year round. These are attractive when covered with contact paper, or spray-painted. You may add decals from Christmas cards and make them seasonal containers. These are projects to start in early Advent so that they will be ready to contain the finished product.

Ginger-Bread Boys

Mom or Dad will need help with this project—perhaps some small hands to place raisin eyes, or a child to sample the first batch. There is no need for fancy outline icing. In making projects simple, we avoid frazzled nerves and frustrated little people.

These cookies delight persons from 9 months of age to 99 years of age, so how can you miss by sharing them with anyone?

Have you remembered to leave a box of these cookies at the county jail? It's a small way of giving hope and saying that you care.

Ingredients:
- ½ cup shortening
- ½ cup sugar
- ½ cup molasses
- ¼ cup milk
- 3 cups flour
- 1 tsp. baking soda
- 1 tsp. salt
- 2 tsps. pumpkin pie spice

Preheat oven to 375°. Combine ingredients and roll the batter to desired thickness; cut out with cookie cutter. Decorate with raisins for eyes and mouth. Place on ungreased cookie sheet. Bake about 8 minutes. Longer baking will make crisp cookies; less baking makes soft cookies. Makes 3 dozen.

Mashed Potato Fudge

This recipe produces a fudge which is a bit less sweet and which will be a welcome delight among your holiday candies.

You will need the sparkling clean, buttered hands of your children to assist you with this one.

Ingredients:

- 3 squares of unsweetened chocolate
- 4 tbsps. margarine
- 1/3 cup unseasoned mashed potatoes (not instant)
- 1/8 tsp. salt
- 1 tsp. vanilla
- 1 1/2 lbs. powdered sugar

Melt together the chocolate and margarine, preferably in a double boiler. Add the rest of the ingredients, except the sugar, and stir until blended. Very slowly add the powdered sugar, making sure that it is gradually but thoroughly worked into the chocolate mixture.

Now, where are our helpers? This mixture must be kneaded until it is shiny and no longer crumbles. Children will enjoy this

119

immensely, and you will have saved yourself a good bit of elbow labor.

Pack down the mixture in a buttered pan. Place walnut pieces on each square that you have scored to cut. Or you may roll the mixture into small balls, with crushed nuts.

Don't lose this recipe! There will be many requests for it as your children grow older.

CHRISTMAS WRAPPING

There are as many ways to wrap packages as there are packages to be wrapped. Children love to participate in this endeavor but they are not always able to make the tight corners and to wrap as securely as we would like. This does not mean that they should not have a part, however.

While the child is cutting designs from cards or even pictures from Christmas catalogs and magazines, carefully wrap your package in a plain-colored paper or white shelving paper.

Show the child where to paste the cut-out on each gift box. You will have original wrapping, and your children will share in the joy of giving. Add a ribbon and a name tag, and the recipient will enjoy the thoughtfulness of your child's personal touch as well as your gift.

Birthday Cake

Christmas is Christ's birthday. When we celebrate our birthdays we usually have a cake with candles, and children expect this as part of the celebration.

It's hard to think of another cake for Christmas when we have been baking for weeks, preparing our holiday feast. However, whether you purchase it or make it from scratch, a birthday cake for Baby Jesus will reap more rewards than any amount of fruitcake or traditional Christmas fare.

If you have little children, let them decorate the cake with small ornaments, a tiny crèche, colored candies, etc. Let it be *their* cake, and, of course, it must have candles. Everyone can join in the singing of "Happy Birthday," and the children should, of course, be the ones to blow out the candles!

Make this an annual event and it will follow your children into adulthood. One more happy memory which helps to penetrate a young child's mind with the true meaning of Christmas.

A Gift of Talent

We all have a very special talent. Each of us has received from God an ability to excel in one field or another. Yet, too often we forget that talents are to be shared. Christmas allows us an excellent opportunity to bring home this fact to our children.

To give a gift to the Christ Child is a wish of every child. Just as the drummer boy brought his music, so too, each child must be encouraged and challenged to prepare something which is a true gift of love—a personal gift for Baby Jesus.

Perhaps this could be a:

- drawing or a painting
- Christmas story or poem
- song practiced for the occasion
- Christmas song well practiced on an instrument
- dance step learned in classes.

There are so many possibilities, and the children know best what they enjoy doing. Many can do simple baking for a needy neighbor. A child with handsome penmanship could write cards for those less endowed. Whatever the talent, each child has been blessed, and this gift should be returned to the Child Jesus with a showing of what we have done with it.

Ask each child to cut from a magazine, or draw a picture pertaining to his or her own talent, sign his or her name on the picture and glue it to a piece of soft fabric. These can be placed in the crib or just beside it as a presentation.

To arrive at our goal of keeping the children close to the Infant Jesus requires putting them in direct association with him who can perfectly understand the mind and feelings of a child.

CHRISTMAS CAROLS

History tells us that until the time of St. Francis of Assisi, there was not a great deal of reference to Christ as a Holy Babe.

Through Francis' teachings and profound love for the Child Jesus, the fourteenth-century followers of this saint began writing verse and music on this theme.

Carols may be defined as religious songs, less formal than the usual church hymns, but inspired by devotional sentiment and intended to be sung outside the church walls.

In the early centuries, choral groups gathered around the Christmas Crib, and included dancing in their tribute to the newborn Babe.

Although it depicts truly an English custom, so many of our greeting cards still show the carolers standing under a lighted street lamp singing carols. I am happy that there are still small groups who carol. It is such a simple thing and yet everyone enjoys it immensely, even those who must trudge through the cold to do it.

When our children were in early grade school, my husband and I took them caroling. I remember wading through a fresh snow storm over unshoveled sidewalks. When the season came the next year we had others joining us. We still receive messages of how much these visits meant to others, and we know how much it meant to us.

Why not try it this year? Vocal excellence and perfect pitch are not necessary. Carol books are available anywhere and make it possible to bring the joy of Christmas to private homes, nursing homes, etc. Both the singer and the listener will experience the warmth of the newborn Babe.

✳✳✳✳✳✳✳✳✳
CHRISTMAS
PLAY

Remember the excitement of the Christmas program? There were skits, tableaus and the singing of carols. That was the one day you had no problem going to school.

One year our local parochial school had its Christmas program in the evening so that the parents could be present. Unfortunately, our daughter had a temperature of 102° that night. But being Santa's helper in the skit, there was no way we could keep her home.

There was a short play done by second-graders. Groups of the children were the angels, several were shepherds, and of course, there were the main celebrities, Mary, Joseph and the Christ Child. Cardboard structures became inns, hotels, etc. Joseph knocked on all the doors seeking shelter, but to no avail. Finally, he turned to Mary and said, "Well, Mary, I guess we'll have to go and find a barn some place." The dialogue was so simple. It had been written by the second-graders themselves. The audience loved it, the children loved it and undoubtedly, our Lord loved it.

Formal written dialogue isn't needed. Instead, words consistent with the vocabulary and speech abilities of the children are most effective. Let the children speak

the lines as they would say them to each other. You will have a Christmas play far superior to any written dialogue by a playwright, and cast and audience alike will have enjoyed their Christmas program.

The following script may be useful for ideas:

A Christmas Play

by Sr. M. Leonella, I.H.M.

All the girls except "Mary" may be dressed as angels. Old sheets make good angel costumes. These could be tied with a piece of cord or colored yarn. If you are creative, let yourself go for a set of "wings."

All the boys except the "kings" and "innkeepers" may be dressed as shepherds. Gunnysacks make good shepherd costumes. You might want to dye an old sheet to make a robe for a king or innkeeper. This would be tied at the waist with a cord. For the head, use a piece of material (any color will serve the purpose) tied with yarn or an old tie. Kings, of course, will wear paper crowns.

Stage Props:

A. A scroll tacked to any kind of support, saying:
"Caesar says: All must register
in their ancestors' city."

B. Three very large boxes, standing side by side, with doors cut out of them. A child stands behind each with a flashlight.

C. A stable made of cardboard, supported by several wooden boards. One spotlight.

Act 1

Mary and Joseph reading the decree from Caesar.

Joseph: Mary, this is an order from Caesar. We must go to Bethlehem because we are of the House of David.

Mary: That's all right, Joseph. God will take care of us. It is written that the Savior will come of the House of David. We are of the House of David.

Joseph: I am sorry that you must travel so far, Mary, just when your Baby is to be born.

Mary: Joseph, God loves us. He will take care of us.

Children sing: "O Come, O Come, Emmanuel."

Act 2

Mary and Joseph seeking shelter at the inns of Bethlehem.

Joseph: Will you give us shelter for the night?

Innkeeper No. 1: No! There is no room!

Mary *(to Joseph):* Joseph, do not be troubled. God, our loving Father, is taking care of us.

Innkeeper No. 2: No! We are crowded.

Joseph: Mary, we will try again. The inns are crowded with pilgrims. Someone will surely give us shelter.

Mary: Joseph, God is with us. He will take care of all our needs.

Innkeeper No. 3: We do not have room here, but I know of a stable in the hills where the shepherds sometimes go.

Joseph: Thank you. May God reward you.

Mary: Let us go, Joseph. My Child is to be born.

Children sing: "Away in a Manger."

Act 3

Shepherds on the hills.

Shepherd No. 1: This night is so different. The stars are like fires in the sky.

Shepherd No. 2: There is one star so bright and so big that I can hardly look at it, and yet I cannot take my eyes from it.

Shepherd No. 3: Our Father in heaven is telling us something. This night is different from all other nights. Something wonderful is to happen.

Angels appear: All sing (from the Mass) Glory to God in the highest.

Angel: This day a Savior is born. He is Christ the Lord. Go to Bethlehem and you will see the Infant lying in a manger. He is wrapped in swaddling clothes. His Mother, Mary, is with him. St. Joseph is there, too.

All sing: "O Come, All Ye Faithful."

After the angels disappear:

Shepherd No. 1: Come, let us go to Bethlehem to see the Savior. God has shown us his great love and mercy.

Act 4

The manger, with the shepherds kneeling around it.
All sing: "Silent Night."
The Wise Men enter, bringing their gifts.

King No. 1: Dear Infant King, I bring you gold because You are King of all men's hearts forever and ever.

King No. 2: Adorable Infant, I give You frankincense because You are Lord of the world and You alone we adore.

King No. 3: Loving Infant, I bring You myrrh because You alone are worthy to be obeyed above all others.

All the children (choral verse):

As the wonderful story of Christmas
Is told in its beauty once more
May the pleasure and joy that it brings us
Be greater than ever before....
May all of God's infinite blessings
Of peace, contentment and cheer
Remain after Christmas is over
To brighten each day of the year.

auline BOOKS & MEDIA

CALIFORNIA
3908 Sepulveda Blvd., Culver City, CA 90230; 310-397-8676
5945 Balboa Ave., San Diego, CA 92111; 619-565-9181
46 Geary Street, San Francisco, CA 94108; 415-781-5180

FLORIDA
145 S.W. 107th Ave., Miami, FL 33174; 305-559-6715

HAWAII
1143 Bishop Street, Honolulu, HI 96813; 808-521-2731

ILLINOIS
172 North Michigan Ave., Chicago, IL 60601; 312-346-4228

LOUISIANA
4403 Veterans Memorial Blvd., Metairie, LA 70006; 504-887-7631

MASSACHUSETTS
50 St. Paul's Ave., Jamaica Plain, Boston, MA 02130; 617-522-8911
Rte. 1, 885 Providence Hwy., Dedham, MA 02026; 617-326-5385

MISSOURI
9804 Watson Rd., St. Louis, MO 63126; 314-965-3512

NEW JERSEY
561 U.S. Route 1, Wick Plaza, Edison, NJ 08817; 732-572-1200

NEW YORK
150 East 52nd Street, New York, NY 10022; 212-754-1110
78 Fort Place, Staten Island, NY 10301; 718-447-5071

OHIO
2105 Ontario Street, Cleveland, OH 44115; 216-621-9427

PENNSYLVANIA
9171-A Roosevelt Blvd., Philadelphia, PA
19114; 215-676-9494

SOUTH CAROLINA
243 King Street, Charleston, SC 29401; 803-577-0175

TENNESSEE
4811 Poplar Ave., Memphis, TN 38117; 901-761-2987

TEXAS
114 Main Plaza, San Antonio, TX 78205; 210-224-8101

VIRGINIA
1025 King Street, Alexandria, VA 22314; 703-549-3806

CANADA
3022 Dufferin Street, Toronto, Ontario, Canada M6B 3T5; 416-781-9131
1155 Yonge Street, Toronto, Ontario, Canada M4T 1W2; 416-934-3440